There's Nothing We Can't Do

Dana Anderson-Helstrom

There's Nothing We Can't Do

Parenting through Childhood Cancer from a Special Educator

WISE INK

ISBN 13: 978-1-63489-480-7
Library of Congress Catalog Number has been applied for.
Printed in the United States of America
First Printing: 2022

26 25 24 23 22 5 4 3 2 1

Cover design by Jason Anscomb
Interior design by Jack Walgamuth

WISE INK

Wise Ink Creative Publishing
807 Broadway St NE
Suite 46
Minneapolis, MN, 55413

This book, like this story, was written by me and Tucker. We dedicate it to Lisa Leininger, my older sister, who is the protector of every member of our family. Lisa provided knowledge, expertise, strength, protection, and fierce love every day of this battle. For her "Tucker Judd," as only she calls him, she brought smiles, motivation, positivity, calm, treatment, and love. She was by our sides and held our hands every step of our journey. A gift I can never aptly explain but will always treasure.

Prologue

After an excellent and easy childhood—happily married parents, fun and loving siblings, easy time in school, and healthy, happy family and friends—I was surprised that life could get so difficult.

In my twenties, I started my "happily-ever-after plan" of finishing graduate school and getting married to my college boyfriend. Two years later, as I was getting excited to start a family, I instead found myself in marital counseling and at Al-Anon meetings, struggling to save the relationship. When I came home on a Thursday night after coaching a high school soccer game to find a goodbye note and a floppy disk of my documents, I was in shock—I would be divorced, and even worse still childless, at age twenty-seven. During this same period, my first job as a school psychologist found me working for a horrible principal. Eventually, I reported to human resources; being naïve and idealistic, I expected it to get him fired. Instead, he went on to make my professional life miserable and interfere with my ability to help students.

Still single at thirty, I was also frustrated with my career choice. Rather than getting more time to help students as I wanted, I was stuck doing intelligence testing and writing reports. My plan to serve as a pillar of the community over a thirty-year career at one school was already over, and worse, I still wasn't a mom yet.

I could fix the career dilemma: I went back to college and got my special education teaching license in the area of emotional and behavioral disorders. I loved working with these kids—well, most of them—and always went the extra mile for them. The becoming-a-mom goal, however, became even more distant after a long-term relationship ended because I wanted to have children and he didn't want any more. To make matters worse, I had to say goodbye to his son, whom I loved dearly. I was devastated once again.

It was then that my mom started encouraging me to become a foster parent. She knew how badly I wanted to be a mother, how I had the right heart and insight to help kids who were emotionally suffering. I very vividly remember telling her, "But I want my own, fresh piece of clay. Not one that has already been molded into a lump. I 'fix' broken kids for a living. I want a child who isn't already hurt and damaged. I want children who don't come with the extra challenges and heartache."

At age thirty-four, I started researching artificial insemination. Maybe I would miss out on marriage, but I was not going to miss out on motherhood. I started saving money with a plan of proceeding with this option on my thirty-fifth birthday. However, at the same time, my mom still thought I should adopt, and I felt selfish for wanting my "own kid" when there were so many kids who needed parents. Ultimately, I decided that I would have one on my own and then perhaps adopt a second child. With that plan in place, I went on to a fun year, leaving any man searches behind. Instead, I bought a cabin on a lake and spent the summer bartending at one of the restaurants that all the locals and cabin owners thoroughly enjoyed.

They say it always happens when you aren't looking for it,

and that was true for me too. I met Judd, the son of a coworker of mine. His dad, Gary, lived on the lake and was recently widowed. I was impressed by how Judd came up every weekend to visit his dad. Soon he started visiting me too. He was a physical education teacher in the same district, so we continued to see each other in the fall. To both of our surprise, our boating and snowmobiling dates turned into a serious relationship. We both loved working with students, sports, and coaching and had strong commitments to our families.

Speaking of family, Judd's could fit around a card table, and mine needed a large dining room table with all the leaves, a second table next to that, plus a kids' table. Despite these daunting numbers, our shared view of family as essential and our love for each other resulted in an engagement, a pregnancy, and a wedding. I had never planned on being an expecting bride, but an accidental pregnancy at age thirty-five was wonderful news.

Later that year, on November 30, 2006, it finally happened! At age thirty-six, I gave birth to a perfectly healthy little boy, Tucker Judd. Then, at thirty-eight, I had a healthy little girl, Kayci Ann. And I wasn't done yet—two years later I had one more wonderful healthy girl, Siera Daniele. There. I had three children that I could raise in a healthy home, and I wouldn't have to deal with the emotional, learning, or behavioral challenges I had witnessed and worked on over the past eighteen years.

Sadly, I wasn't able to keep my children's lives as perfect as I had intended. Judd and I needed to divorce when they were young. It was a challenge moving three children ages five, four, and two-and-a-half to an apartment in the metro area. Every morning, I still drove the younger two to St. Michael for daycare and preschool, then went back down to Minnetonka with Tucker, who was in kindergarten at the school where I worked as the special education teacher. But I did it, and I was never bitter—I had my kids, and they were all healthy.

Five months later, I moved the four of us into the only house I could afford in Hopkins, where I wanted our kids to attend school. It was a great neighborhood, but the house was dirty and neglected, run by an absentee owner who had rented the upstairs to drug addicts and the downstairs to a family with five young, unsupervised kids. When I was closing on the house, I learned the garage was gone because the city had demolished it some years ago after discovering it was doubling as a meth lab. Before agreeing to close, I was assured by Hopkins city officials that the house was clean from any chemical dangers. It was safe, but nothing anyone I remotely cared about could live in, let alone my children.

After helping me to move my belongings, my parents and sisters came back the next day with every cleaning chemical Menards sold. We scrubbed, scoured, and even sanded the stains off every surface. My dad and I then repaired and painted every wall, ceiling, window frame, door, cupboard, and piece of trim in the entire house, which required four gallons of spackle and thirty-five gallons of paint. My parents and I continued to work around the clock for weeks, and by September I was living in an adorable, historic house with my three amazing kids. Kayci and Siera were set in their pink and purple room with bunk beds; Tucker's room was painted in the official colors of the Minnesota Twins and covered with baseball décor. However, as much as Tucker loved the look of his room, he insisted on sleeping on the trundle bed in his sisters' room. He always wanted to be next to Kayci and watching over Siera. I was grateful every day for how much my three children loved each other.

Life was great. I loved our healthy, happy TKSD foursome (Tucker/Kayci/Siera/Dana). Our commute was down from an hour to ten minutes; we were fifteen minutes away from my parents and siblings; we had the perfect school for Tucker and Kayci, where I was so proud to work, and an amazing preschool for Siera; and the kids were in outstanding baseball, hockey, and gymnastics programs. I didn't want for anything, but fate gave me more.

I met Kevin that fall. We instantly became friends, then started dating, and after ten months we were serious enough for him to meet the most important people in my life. Tucker and Siera instantly bonded with Kevin; Kayci was more skeptical of anyone entering our foursome. However, slowly but surely, we were becoming a group of five. As I told my dad, "My three kids and I are the perfect cake—I can't believe I am lucky enough to have the frosting now too!" Kevin and I were looking at rings and making plans. Finally, at age forty-six, after a couple decades of struggles, my adult life was about to be perfect.

Chapter One

Like most kids, mine love Halloween. Tucker was extra excited for Halloween 2015 because, now that he was almost nine years old, I'd allowed him to have a scary costume for the first time. Our favorite tradition was bringing the grandchildren to my dad's office downtown, where he showed them off to his coworkers. Papa was overjoyed every time he saw his grandchildren, which was at least weekly, but this day was his favorite since he'd had grandkids. This year Halloween was on a Saturday, so the kids went to Papa's office on Friday, the 30th. I wasn't able to go, so my younger sister and brother, Sara and Ryan, brought my kids along with their own four.

When I picked up Tucker, Kayci, and Siera, Sara mentioned that Tucker's knee might have twisted or something, because toward the end of the day he'd started to limp. Tucker's knee had been hurting for four weeks now, requiring ibuprofen for the past three. The week before, I had brought him to his new pediatrician, who'd thought it was a ligament strain and told us to keep him out of sports for a couple weeks to rest it. That was a big ask, but we did it—hockey season was just starting, and after four months of baseball, Tucker was excited for the next four months to be full of hockey and friends.

The following day, the kids and I left midday for Judd's house in St. Michael so they could play with their friends before trick-or-treating. The previous year, Tucker had left our group to go door-to-door with his best friend Jack, too big to stick with his mom and little sisters. I anticipated this year would be the same. Until it wasn't.

By the time we finished the group pictures with all the neighborhood kids, Tucker told me his knee hurt too much to walk on. I told him, "Just don't go as far," thinking he meant he wouldn't be able to do the usual ninety minutes.

But Tucker clarified, "No, Mom. It hurts too much to walk *at all.* I'm going to stay at the house with Dad and hand out candy."

My heart broke for him that evening. When the girls and I returned, Tucker still couldn't walk. I couldn't bear him missing out on the entire night, so I ended up carrying him through the two backyards over to Jack's house. *Wow,* I thought to myself, *these seem a lot bigger when carrying a seventy-pound person.* By the time I arrived with Tucker in my arms, all the kids had already picked out the orange suckers, Starbursts, and Skittles and put them into a pile for him. Tucker loved Halloween but hated chocolate.

Halloween night was the first of many times I, at age forty-six, would carry my nearly nine-year-old boy.

All weekend I was giving Tucker children's liquid ibuprofen, the orange kind, but he still couldn't put any weight on his right leg. On Monday, November 2, I used the referral the pediatrician had given to me "just in case." For what would turn out to be the first of many times, I politely but firmly advocated with medical personnel for my son and secured an appointment for later that afternoon with the pediatric orthopedic specialist. I later found out how "special" this doctor truly was.

It was easy to go get Tucker for this appointment because he was right down the hall in his third-grade classroom. I loved working at the same school that my children attended. The International Spanish Language Academy, which is lovingly called ISLA, is a charter school featuring full Spanish immersion and the International Baccalaureate Primary Years Programme. There are two classrooms of students in each grade, kindergarten through sixth.

Tucker's younger sister and true best friend, Kayci, was in her second-grade classroom right next door to his. I poked my head in and told her that Papa would be picking her up after school, and that I was bringing Tucker to the doctor to "fix his knee." Next, I walked down the hall to Siera's kindergarten classroom. I gave her a hug and told her that Kayci would pick her up from the classroom and Papa would bring them home. Papa and Grandma are my parents by title, but in reality they're so much more—my rocks, coparents, and foundation.

Then I went to get Tucker. Since he still couldn't bear weight on his right leg, I brought my office chair to his classroom and wheeled him to the employees' entrance in the back of the school (there may or may not have been a few crazy spins on the way down the hall), then carried him the rest of the way to my minivan. My muscles strained, but my heart hurt more; when I jostled his leg and his knee had to bend, he would cry out in pain.

During the drive from Minnetonka to St. Paul, I talked with Tucker and told him how great it was that we'd be seen today, so we could get the pain figured out and fixed in time for the upcoming hockey season. Despite having to sit out tryouts, he'd still made the top team of Mite 4 since the coaches knew he was a great player, an even better teammate, and incredibly coachable. Every coach wanted Tucker on his team, and all kids wanted him as a teammate. I used to think I was a biased mom, but I would come to learn that indeed, Tucker truly was a special person, one that everyone wanted to be around.

I was not lucky enough to find a parking spot close to the entrance of Gillette Children's Specialty Healthcare Center, so I just carried Tucker to the door. There were a few times in this jaunt that I nearly dropped my son. It was terrifying—Tucker was slipping out of my arms while trying so hard to not cry out in pain. He was a boy who worried as much, if not more, about other people as he did himself. This was especially true of how he treated his mom.

Thankfully, an adrenaline surge like the ones you see in cartoons and read about in emergencies hit me; I was able to carry him to the doors, which, thank goodness, were automatic. As my back and arm muscles seized up, I was even more grateful that the security guard saw my strain and jumped to get Tucker a wheelchair. I used my last ounce of physical strength to try to gently place him onto the seat, but I am sure there were a few inches of "free fall." The pain on Tucker's face confirmed that.

At that moment, I said, "There, the worst is over! Now we just get to wheel you around and get this knee fixed!" That was the first and only time it was "fun" for Tucker to ride in a wheelchair, but it was definitely not the only time he would be in one. The worst was not over. It hadn't even begun.

Dr. Koop was kind, old, and very thorough. He spent thirty minutes with us, having both of us re-explain the details of Tucker's pain and the incident we thought had caused it five weeks ago, when going down a slide had gone wrong. We also kept reiterating Tucker's sports schedule—he had been busy since September, when fall baseball overlapped with preseason hockey. I told Dr. Koop how Tucker had started needing ibuprofen every evening for four weeks, then afternoons and evenings the following week, and then all day starting two weeks ago. That was when I had brought him to the pediatrician who figured it was possible ligament damage.

We left Dr. Koop's office with orders to go get a full leg stabilizer and an appointment for an MRI the following day. I was really impressed how he was able to get us an appointment so quickly. I thought, *Wow, when doctors from Gillette Children's want something, people really jump to get it done!* Growing up in the Twin Cities area, I had always heard how outstanding Gillette Children's Hospital was, so I was thankful that Tucker's pediatrician had referred him to the best.

While we were in the waiting area, I noticed the severity of the afflictions of most of the children around us. Once again, I immediately thought how lucky I was to have healthy children. *Some families really have to go through a LOT,* I thought to myself. The two weeks without sports was seeming like a great problem to have. I left full of gratitude that all my son had was a sports or slide injury.

Although I thought it was likely a minor problem, I did insist to Judd that we take Tucker to his MRI like Dr. Koop had scheduled. On Tuesdays, the kids usually went to Judd's house for the evening, so he wanted to reschedule; instead, all five of us went to the appointment. I was surprised that it would take fifty minutes for the imaging to happen, and horrified that I wasn't going to be allowed in the room to stay beside my son. How was a little eight-year-old boy supposed to handle such a scary new thing without his mother holding his hand? How was a mom supposed to sit in a waiting room for so long away from her child?

I hated the wait, but not as much as the girls did. Seven-year-old Kayci and five-year-old Siera were more than bored. Attending to them made the time go even slower. Now all three of my children were miserable, and I couldn't fix it. That was a position I hated, but soon would be the situation in which I found myself constantly.

At 11:37 the following morning, Wednesday, November 4, I received a message from Dr. Koop himself, asking to please call him at my "very earliest convenience." That didn't sound good—*I better go outside to make this call,* I thought, *just in case it's something bad like a break in a growth plate.* I wanted to be able to swear if needed.

At 11:39, I made the call that changed my life forever.

As a mother of three little kids and as a school psychologist, I have called many doctors' and therapists' offices, and every time I've had to leave a message with the receptionist or nurse's desk. Not this time. After I stated my name, before I could finish the sentence—"I am returning Dr. Koop's . . ."—the receptionist replied, "I will get Dr. Koop right away."

How odd. And how ominous. Why would *he* need to talk to me? And why did the receptionist spring into action when she heard my name?

By 11:40, I was talking to Dr. Koop. There was no small talk.

"Dana, I am really sorry to have to tell you this news." The punch to my stomach from the voicemail flared as though Mike Tyson had thrown it. "I am afraid that Tucker has osteosarcoma. That is a very rare cancer of the bone."

If I were normal, I would now tell you that I didn't hear, remember, or understand what came next. But I am not normal. At the time I didn't know this about myself, but I have the ability to galvanize and be a fact finder. It makes sense; I have dealt with bad news from so many students and families over my twenty years in special education. However, I didn't know I could do that when talking about my own child.

"So now what?" I asked robotically. "Where do I bring him and what are the next steps?" Despite my brain still working well, my legs were giving out, so I sat down on a large rock, failing to notice it was rounded and not at all conducive to sitting.

"There are two places that deal with osteosarcoma. Like I said, it is very rare. They are the U of M Masonic Children's Hospital in Minneapolis and the Mayo Clinic in Rochester," Dr. Koop replied.

"Which one is better? Or should I go to both? Who should I call for an appointment?" I asked. I thought I should go inside the school to get paper, but my legs couldn't move.

"If he were my grandson, I would bring him to Masonic. The orthopedic surgeon there is the best in his field, and I don't just say that because he is a friend. He is simply the best."

"OK, I trust you. [Who wouldn't trust someone who said he would bring his grandson there?] What is the number I should call?" Again, my mouth was saying all the right things, but my brain was trying to remind me that I was sitting in a parking lot, not at a desk—I couldn't write this stuff down, and there was no way I was going to remember a phone number.

Dr. Koop must have known that no mother could remember phone numbers or appointment dates when given this news. Luckily, he was excellent at relaying the worst information. "I hope you don't mind, but I already called Dr. Clohisy." (Galvanized or not, I would not remember how to say that name for a couple days.) "You have an appointment to see him at 3:00 p.m.

on Friday. I also sent over the MRI film already and discussed it with him."

"Does he think this is osteo . . . whatever you said?" I could not bring myself to say the "c" word and couldn't remember the long word.

"Yes, Dr. Clohisy has seen the film and believes it is osteosarcoma. Like I said, it is a very rare cancer that attacks the bone. Tucker's right femur shows it in the MRI. But it can only be confirmed with a biopsy."

"So, it might NOT be osteo?" I asked with the utmost hope.

"It is very unlikely that it is not osteosarcoma." Tyson just kept punching me. I couldn't feel my legs or arms, but the blows to my stomach were excruciating.

"What else should I do? What other appointments does Tucker need? Should I set up the biopsy?"

"I already discussed this with Dr. Clohisy. He made room in his schedule to do the biopsy first thing Monday morning, November 9."

This was the first time the news brought me relief and pain simultaneously. *Yay! They got my son in right away! Shit! Why did they feel the need to make room in his schedule? This must be really bad!* By then I was one with the rock; I couldn't feel where it ended and I began. I just kept talking, a rock with a stomachache, holding a phone in a parking lot while the cold November wind blew.

"Dr. Koop, you keep saying how 'rare' this is. What does that mean?"

"Very rare," he answered solemnly.

"I need to know what that means. What are the numbers?"

"In all the patients I see, I have to make this phone call about twice a year."

"Oh. And do kids survive this?" *Please say yes, of course, very treatable.*

"It is a very challenging cancer. But Dr. Clohisy and I think we caught it early, so there is good reason to be hopeful."

That translated in my mind to, "*Yes, Tucker will survive this.*" I am a very determined person, and I work to get what I want. I don't give up, and as Tucker's mom I would see him through this. *I will not let Kayci and Siera lose their brother. I will do everything right and get my child better.* To use my favorite phrase, "I will fix this!"

I'd thought I had already had enough misfortune, but apparently I was not done. Apparently, I was not only supposed to conquer the challenges of two divorces, fighting for custody, a contentious relationship with my children's father, challenges at work, and financial problems. I was also put on this earth to beat this "osteo" thing with my firstborn child, while keeping my healthy children in focus too and taking care of their mental health. *OK, well, then that is what I will do. There really is no choice in the matter.*

Now I had to go back inside the school to begin this journey, which I would later realize was a war. My "decision" to not let this kill my son was the energy I needed to morph back into a human and get off the rock. I could stand now because I had to go take care of my son and get rid of his cancer.

I walked in without shedding a tear, for two reasons. One, I was in shock. Two, there were children around, including my three. Right now this was my problem, not theirs. I walked to my office and told my officemate and friend, Moria, that I was going to be out in the staff parking lot; I asked her to send my friend Dayra, who was the dean of students, back there to meet me. Moria didn't know what to say; she asked if everything was OK, and I replied, "No. I need to leave. Please go get Dayra."

Then Moria asked if I wanted my coat and started to hand it to me. I stared at her blankly and asked why I would want it. She said, "Because it's cold out, and you look cold. Your hands and nose are red." Just then, I realized I hadn't noticed. To this day, I remember the exact words of the phone call, where the landscaping rocks were, which window I was standing beside, but I cannot remember feeling cold.

But I accepted my coat from Moria. "OK," I said, and went back outside. Then I called Kevin and told him to not ask me any questions, just to come pick me up and bring me to my parents' house, which thankfully was only twelve minutes away.

Dayra, my dear Colombian friend, met me in back. She asked what was wrong, and I said the words: "Tucker has cancer."

Though it wasn't loud, I knew her ears could hear me—but her mind and positive spirit couldn't. "No, he doesn't. Dana, you are imagining the worst."

So I said it louder. "Dayra, Tucker has cancer. I just got off the phone with the doctor."

"No, honey. It is something else," she insisted.

My entire protective shield shattered. "Tucker has fucking cancer! The doctor just told me! I am leaving now and Kevin is bringing me to my parents' house. Please call them and tell them to sit there and wait for me!"

I had never before or since sworn at sweet Dayra. The poor woman was in tears. Tucker had been her student when he was in first grade. She loved him dearly.

My assistant principal and Moria also came out there, which was good—Dayra needed support, not only from the news but from seeing a side of me that I had never shown to a friend, especially not one as sweet as her. Luckily, I regained my composure despite being in shock. I restated the three words, calmly this time. The women reached out to hug me.

Backing away, I told them sternly, "NO ONE MUST KNOW! My son has five carefree days left of his childhood, and *nothing* will change that!"

They agreed, and then I got into Kevin's car.

Chapter Two

We rode in silence. I needed that time to calm myself and regain my strength. I was not going to allow myself to have another outburst like I had with Dayra.

I told Kevin that I must first share this news with my parents. They had always been the people I wanted to tell my good news first, and definitely who I turned to in bad times. In this book's introduction, I mentioned how my challenging adulthood was in sharp contrast to my wonderful childhood. I grew up in a very close family. I was the middle child of five and am one of few people who can say she has "one of each": an older sister, an older brother, a younger sister, and a younger brother. Mom and Dad always put family first, and we kids benefitted more than we ever realized. There was never a time they weren't there to celebrate our victories or console us in our troubles.

As we five children grew older, we didn't split off when we started new families. Instead, we were lucky enough to have in-laws and grandchildren grow into our family, which has been nicknamed "the A-Team" since the 1980s, when we were brainstorming a personalized license plate for the Ford van we took on our many family road trips. ("Andersons" didn't fit.) The A-Team had grown from the seven of us to twenty-two and was stronger than ever. We all lived within twenty minutes of my parents, who were still in our childhood home in Bloomington.

Now that home would be the site where I told the matriarch and patriarch that one of the youngest members of the A-Team was the first to be struck with the beast that is cancer. I couldn't imagine how much this would devastate them. They were very healthy, and I have no doubt they would have given ANYTHING to have it be one of them instead of their sweet, funny, and loving little grandson. The intense pain in my stomach returned as Kevin pulled into their driveway.

I walked in and up the six stairs to the living room. My dad wanted to hug me, but I walked over to the couch and sat down—a hug would have broken me. Mom sat down while Dad stayed standing, next to her chair. I knew they would be so worried about everyone, so I decided to spare them some pain and stay strong.

I calmly explained that Dr. Koop had called, and that apparently Tucker's knee pain had nothing to do with sports or slides or ligaments. Instead, his lower right femur was full of bone cancer. I already knew how to pronounce the word: osteosarcoma. I think I actually said the words, "The good news is . . ." showing how much I didn't want them to worry about me. I explained we had caught it early, so if I just made sure to get Tucker through this, we would be fine.

Whew, I made it through that. A few tears, but I successfully hid my fear and pain.

Then Sara walked up the stairs.

Ugh! Now I had to say it all over again. Sara asked what was wrong, so I restarted my speech. This time, when I said "bone cancer," Sara erupted into tears and came over and held me. "I am so sorry, Dana. This is your nightmare coming true."

These words broke me down, and my tears came pouring out. *What the hell? My little boy has cancer.*

Sara knew that my biggest fear in life was my children getting cancer. As soon as Tucker was born, I'd started donating to St. Jude's Children Cancer Fund. I used a personal day every year to help at the phone banks during their telethon. I had my students make cards and send them to the children at St. Jude's. Every time anything bad happened to me, I reminded myself, "At least my kids don't have cancer." I have no idea why this was such a fear of mine. The moment Sara said that, nine years of fear surged. She was right; my worst nightmare was happening.

My phone rang, and I was able to snap back into the caretaker/fixer mom. It was Dr. Clohisy's office, confirming the appointments and giving additional information. It was good to regroup and get back to the task of getting rid of my son's cancer. I learned a lot of horrible details talking to Dr. Clohisy. The good news was that he already had a team of doctors in place who had looked at Tucker's MRI. I told him that Dr. Koop had shared that with me and thanked him. Dr. Clohisy asked me if I understood that biopsy meant surgery. I said no. He informed me that the surgery would last one to two hours, as they would be taking a biopsy of the bone and the tissue around it.

I asked about a body scan to see if the cancer had spread. Dr. Clohisy said yes, Tucker would need one, but we wouldn't know when that would be until we made a plan. I didn't ask about chemo or radiation because I didn't think it was a given. That was a naïve thought. I asked how common or rare osteosarcoma was. Dr. Clohisy had a very nice answer: "For us, it is very common. It's what we do every day." But he went on to admit, "It is a very rare tumor." For Tucker it was even more rare, because it normally appears in boys between the ages of fourteen and twenty-five, when rapid growth is happening. Tucker wasn't even nine yet and was of average height.

Just then, Lisa, my older sister, walked in. Anderson women are strong, but Lisa is Hercules. She is the oldest of the five children, a mother of three, and a physical therapist at Abbott Northwestern Hospital for over twenty-five years. Lisa has been taking care of all A-Team members' medical worries since I was in high school. As I repeated, for the third time, that Tucker had cancer, she instantly jumped into action, reviewing my notes and answering questions all of us had about logistics. Her experience and knowledge were amazing resources for all of us, at that moment and for the rest of the entire journey. It felt wonderful to be assured by her that we had this and that she would be attending the appointment with me and Tucker on Friday.

My head was swimming with all this information, but I knew I had another major task to do. I had to inform Judd. We had been divorced for two-and-a-half years by then and still didn't get along well. We tried to hide that from our children, but our families were nonetheless aware. I wanted Judd to hear the news in person, not endure a phone call like I had. I knew I wasn't the one who he would want consoling him, so I called the person he would: his older sister and only sibling Kris. I had her taken out of a meeting so I could tell her the news. Their mother had died from breast cancer eleven years earlier, so I knew Tucker's diagnosis would be even scarier for them to hear.

I gave every piece of information I had to Kris. She was not only the matriarch of the Helstrom family now, but also a very intelligent and caring person. I asked her to please drive up to Judd's house and tell him when he got home from work. She agreed this would be best and made her plan. I was so glad

Judd would not be alone when he got the news, and that he would have help calling his father, Gary, who was a heartbroken widower. I knew he would tremble at the thought of his only grandson being struck with cancer.

By this time, it was 2:30 p.m. I told all assembled I had to get going back to ISLA. Mom told me to stay there and take some time. "No," I replied, "I am going to get some eye drops from the closet and then have Kevin drive me back to ISLA right now."

"What?!" they all exclaimed pretty much in unison. "Why?"

"Because my children are there and come to my office every day after school. If I'm not there, they're going to ask if something is wrong and then worry. My children have only five days left of childhood innocence. Five more days where Tucker's biggest worry is whether the Minnesota Wild hockey team is going to win and his biggest burden is having to read twenty minutes a night. I am NOT going to let anything take away a single minute of their childhood innocence before they have to start worrying about cancer, pain, and death. None of us are going to take that away from them. Therefore, we will act 'normal' and be happy around all of the grandchildren. Let's give all of them these five days to be carefree kids."

Everyone agreed. I put drops in my eyes, and Kevin drove me back. At three o'clock, I was in my office making sure everything was in place for about fifteen minutes from now, when my beautiful children walked in. Well, two of them walked in—Tucker still had his "temporary" wheelchair for getting through the halls. I worked extra hard to not show sadness when he wheeled into my office; I still told myself in a couple days he would be done with that thing. If only that were true.

Chapter Three

I barely remember the first full day after the news, but I do remember my new reality being what I called a "fishbowl." As I had sole physical custody, my children were with me all but two evenings a week and every other weekend, when they went to Judd's house. Thus, most of the time, I was with my kids twenty-four hours a day. All four of us were together at ISLA, home, and each child's sports activities. With Tucker in so much pain, he was also sleeping in my bed every night so that I could massage his leg and get him ibuprofen throughout the night.

Even school days, while the children were in their classrooms, were not a time for me to emote or even talk about this new reality, because my office was right across from the student bathrooms—any one of their friends could see me at any time. I was not going to let my kids hear from someone else that their mom looked sad or was talking about doctors. Thus, I was in a fishbowl, always on display to my children and/or their peers, leaving me no choice but to act like everything was fine, all the time. At night, I tucked the girls in and lay with them until they fell asleep. Then I lay next to Tucker, being sure to not make any noise when the tears rolled down my cheek onto my pillow. His face was so beautiful. I stared at it as I caressed his hair, his beautiful blond hair.

I do remember googling "osteosarcoma." I only read one article—I stopped when it stated the disease brought with it a likelihood of amputation. I nearly threw up. My amazingly athletic son's favorite thing to do was play sports with Kayci, his friends, and kids who would soon become his friends. This couldn't happen to my son! He was a little boy who should be running and playing, not fighting cancer and getting a leg cut off! I was so sick to my stomach I shut down my computer and texted my parents and siblings. They gave me great advice: "The internet is not your friend. Only listen to Tucker's doctors because they are the only ones who know his case." It is one of the few times I have never challenged my parents' advice. I did not search the internet again that night, nor ever, which I would later find out was beyond a blessing.

Thursday evening, I told my kids that the following day Tucker had an appointment with someone who would tell us how to make his knee feel better. This would be the second of many, many times Papa or Grandma would pick the girls up from ISLA while Tucker and I were at a medical appointment. When the day arrived, the immobilizer on Tucker's leg made it difficult to manage his wheelchair. It was another part of my new reality: having to carry my son down four front steps to the curb, getting him in and out of his wheelchair, and loading him in and out of my van. While I can't remember it now, I know I lived for months with back pain. However, a mother doesn't dwell on her own pain, only her child's.

Despite my fake upbeat attitude, Tucker was nervous for the doctor's appointment. My son was not even nine years old, but he was already wise and a worrier. Tucker got more suspicious when Aunt Lisa and Aunt Kris showed up at the appointment. I explained to him that helping everyone in the family through their medical concerns was what Lisa did, which was the truth.

Then I told him Kris's office was nearby, so it was a good excuse for her to take a break from work. The lying had begun.

Before the appointment, I had talked with Dr. Clohisy's assistant extensively and told them Tucker was NOT to hear the c-word. I explained that my children had only known one child with cancer, an ISLA student named Adrian, who ended up dying from it. To them, cancer meant death. During our appointment, Dr. Clohisy talked with Tucker matter-of-factly and told him he was going to help him get rid of his pain. He chatted with Tucker about hockey but admitted he didn't follow the Wild. Tucker was happy to fill him in.

After ten minutes, Tucker went to the waiting room with Kris while Judd, Lisa, and I stayed with Dr. Clohisy to ask more questions. My most urgent question was, "Is Tucker going to lose his leg?" I knew he wasn't going to die—I would see to that. But I was terrified of amputation.

Dr. Clohisy gave us good news: we had caught the cancer early. He told us that he expected "treatment to be effective and the cancer to be gone." I noted the wording did not include words like "cured" or "he will be fine." But I didn't want to read into it. Dr. Clohisy went on to say that because the cancer had been caught early and hadn't progressed, he believed Tucker would *not* need to have his leg amputated. He said the tumor had been there for only two to eight weeks. However, it was already ten centimeters long. I was shocked by how fast it had grown.

More scary news was the news that Tucker's femur was compromised because it was no longer a bone—it was a tumor. The cancer had taken away the real bone cells, replacing them with hardened cancer cells that imitated bone. If his femur were to break, the cancer would be released through the body and the leg would need to be amputated. *Can I put Tucker in bubble wrap and keep him inside?* was my immediate thought. No, I couldn't. But I would keep him in the wheelchair with the immobilizer on at all times.

Lisa, Judd, and I hurried out of the room so as to not worry Tucker. He immediately asked, "What's the bad news?"

My boy was very in tune with me, so I knew I had to deliver some type of bad news. Therefore, I told him that his knee was damaged and we couldn't let it suffer further injury. "Dr. Clohisy said you have to stay in the wheelchair with the immobilizer on."

Tucker let out a groan and yelled "NO!" for the first of many times. He was so upset. One day had been "fun," but now the wheelchair made him feel like something was wrong with him and reminded him of missing hockey. I told him he was the most fun kid I knew, so there was no way he wouldn't be able to have fun in the wheelchair. Then I reminded him we had the Dia De Los Muertos Fiesta that night at school, so we had to get going.

For the first time in over forty-eight hours, I didn't have to fake being in a good mood. I actually was feeling happy—I was so relieved that we'd caught the cancer early and that Tucker wouldn't need an amputation. When Judd, who'd gone home after the appointment, texted me how upset he was, I answered, "We get our kid and he gets his leg!" This was the time to be happy.

An hour later, the joyous moment was over when Tucker started crying as we pulled up to ISLA. He did not want to go to a party in a wheelchair. He saw all the kids running on the playground and bounding up the stairs into the school. Normally, Tucker was the kid who disappeared with friends immediately upon arriving, and I had to search for him at the end of any gathering. I would bring him home all sweaty from running around and with a sore stomach from laughing so much.

The girls were so sad to see their brother crying. I haven't described the connection between Tucker and Kayci yet—think Elliot and E.T., and that will come close to explaining it. Kayci felt all the pain Tucker had and also didn't want to go into the party. Luckily, I am a stubborn woman and was not going to let my kids be sad. Tucker had been attending and loving parties since his baby shower when he was two weeks old. When he was four weeks old at his first Christmas, he'd stayed awake all seven hours of the A-Team's Christmas gathering. He was not going to miss his first party on my watch!

Before I could even get him into the wheelchair, his buddies had sprinted over to our van. They argued over who got to push him. I was about to tell them, "None of you!" so I could protect him, but I knew that wasn't the right answer. I picked Jayden to push him, because he idolized Tucker and would never want him to get hurt. Soon I was holding Kayci's and Siera's hands, walking into ISLA, and Tucker was off somewhere with all the kids. This was the first of numerous times I was delighted to see how eight-year-old kids can adapt to change with innocence yet strength. They were not fazed by the wheelchair, nor did they see limitations. Instead they saw their friend and didn't hesitate to continue to have fun with him.

There was a plan for Tucker to sleep at Jayden's house that night for their first sleepover. Both boys were so excited for it, but I was worried because Tucker was still in pain and apparently very fragile. However, he would be more miserable if he missed out on this, so I knew I had to let it happen. I also knew I could trust Jayden's parents, Jake and Alissa, to take care of Tucker as well as I would. They loved him like a son, and both Jayden and his older brother Jackson loved it when Tucker was at their house. Tucker did too. He was a mama's boy and loved his sisters, but he loved the chance to go be with boys. In fact, he called their house his "boy home."

I knew I had to tell Jake what was going on, so I brought him to a quiet hallway. For the first time in forty-eight hours, I had to tell someone the horrible news. I had to see the pain and shock in his eyes. *Damn, I hate hurting people.* I told Jake that I needed him to make sure Tucker did not take off his immobilizer, that he got his ibuprofen, and that he didn't jump around. There are very few people with whom I trust my sick kids, but I knew Jake would be extremely attentive and watch over Tucker the whole time. I then asked him not to tell Alissa. I wanted her to have this one last night of joy watching her sons play with their best friend. Soon enough she would be heartbroken and worried.

That night, I took this opportunity to have both Kayci and Siera sleep in my bed with me. Their lives were about to turn upside down as well, and unlike with Tucker, I wouldn't be able to be next to them the entire time. I put the phone by my pillow in case any calls came, but knew Jake had this. I was sure Alissa was spoiling the boys and that Tucker was laughing, not thinking about his leg. His biggest worry would be how many video games he would be able to play before falling asleep. Just like childhood should be.

Saturday morning, the girls and I picked up Tucker. Kayci

already missed him and wanted to get him at eight o'clock, but we waited until ten. Then I had to bring him to his hockey pictures. This was crippling on the inside, but again, I was going to hide it.

I kept a smile on my face as all the hockey boys flocked around Tucker, excited to finally see him again. The coaches were excited to see Tucker too and came up to me with great anticipation in their voices, asking me when he would be back on the ice. "Not for a little while," I said calmly. "They aren't sure what is wrong with his knee yet, so we have to get it looked at by a specialist." What a euphemism for *"Not this year, because he has cancer!"*

Tucker was so happy to be wearing his Mite 4 jersey. I found an adaptation to include Tucker in the pictures, even though he couldn't pose in skates like everyone else. We got his breezers and hockey socks on over the immobilizer and propped him up leaning on his stick like a studly hockey boy. His smile was so big and so sweet.

I watched from behind the photographer and thought, *I wonder when the next time I see him in hockey gear will be.* I couldn't go there, so I just embarrassed Tucker by telling him how cute he was in front of all his buddies.

Chapter Four

Oh, how I wished I could keep the fun going on Sunday, and not just for Tucker's benefit. I didn't want this whole cancer battle to start. But it had started, without letting us know. Besides, since Tucker was in a lot of pain, I told myself it was a "good thing" to bring him into surgery in the morning. I was worried about that surgery, but what I should have feared was the night before, when Tucker had to be off his pain medication.

During the day, I brought the kids to Toys "R" Us so the girls could buy Tucker a present. I had told them that their brother was having surgery so the doctor could look inside to see what was wrong. To soften their fears, I told them that we always get gifts for surgeries. Kayci and Siera picked out an orange, round little monster guy. Since Tucker was eighteen months old, orange had been not only his favorite color, but also his favorite flavor. He dressed himself in orange, cheered on all college and pro teams that were orange, and ate orange-flavored everything—so fitting, as the color was bright and cheerful just like him. A few years ago, Sara found rocks called orange chalcedony. The sign above them said they "encourage brotherhood among all." How apropos.

Tucker wanted to get the girls something too; I hadn't thought of that, but of course this sweet boy did. He said they would need something to play with so they didn't miss him so much. It was the day before his first surgery, and his chief concern was how his sisters would get through it.

Tucker's last dose of ibuprofen was around noon. He had to be med-free for his 9:00 a.m. surgery. After dinner, we opened the presents and took cute pictures. Tucker started complaining about the pain, so I started massaging and trying ice packs. Then I had to give him a bath with horrible-smelling disinfectant soap. Tucker's nose was like a bloodhound's, and smells triggered his gag reflex. He had strong tastebuds too, which turned out to be extremely problematic throughout the cancer battle as there are many pungent smells and oral medicines. This first bath with the hospital soap foreshadowed all of it. Tucker yelled and cried in the bathtub—the horrible smell, the pain of me having to scrub his sore leg, no ibuprofen left in his system. It was so hard to be inflicting this pain on my son. Again, foreshadowing of so much more to come.

By the time I'd finished the bath and carried Tucker to the couch, he couldn't take any more. It was 9:00 p.m. and he was screaming in intense pain. I tried every calming technique I knew of—essential oils, distraction, massage—but nothing helped, so I grabbed my phone and called my mom.

I am so fortunate to have an amazing, loving, and incredibly wise mother on whom I can always rely for help with parenting. She of course called Lisa, and they were there within minutes. Lisa found Kayci sitting on the floor of her room, wrapped up tight in a ball with her hands over her ears sobbing. She was not only hearing her best friend's pain—she was feeling it with him. Kayci was inconsolable. Siera sat there watching her sister cry and hearing her brother scream. This was the first of many manifestations of cancer's hurt for everyone in the family. I called

Kevin, who lived three houses down, and told him he needed to get the girls out of the house. They could not hear this any longer. Papa had to carry Kayci, who didn't want to leave her brother, and Kevin helped Siera wrap up in her blanket so they could go to his house.

While all that was happening, my mom and I were trying to soothe Tucker, whose eyes were red from tears and throat was sore from yelling. Lisa was on the phone trying to get a hold of any doctor she could. With her medical experience, she knew there was some form of pain medication that was safe before surgery. She was not going to stop until she got a doctor to prescribe it for her nephew. Eventually, she raced off to Walgreens. I can imagine how she drove and what she said if anyone tried to slow her down at the drugstore.

Lisa is a bright sunny day when everything is fine, but if her family member is in pain and needs medical attention, she is an instant hurricane, shattering the glass and slamming against the doors to get whatever her loved one needs. Nine years earlier, she'd been the wind that got me my pain medication after my C-section when the doctor forgot to put it on my chart; three years after that, she'd been the rain that pounded the doctors trying to evict Sara, who was still bleeding heavily after giving birth; on this night, she was the thunder that woke the doctors to get the right pain medication for Tucker.

When Lisa returned with the relief we were all seeking, poor Tucker was in a frenzy, afraid of the taste and smell of the new medicine. Finding patience and understanding for a child who was now afraid of the antidote to what was hurting him was something only a grandmother could do. Grandma held his hand and spoke softly and reassuringly, calming both him and me down; soon after, we got the medication down. I held my boy, rubbing his forehead, kissing his cheeks, whispering distractions into his ears. Finally, Tucker calmed down, caught his breath, and was out of pain.

Two hours of pure hell. But it was over, thanks to the powerful women of the A-Team: Lisa, Mom, and me, with the support of Dad and Kevin to take care of the girls.

When we got the girls back home, Kayci went right over to Tucker on the couch and lay beside him. Only seven years old, but she knew how to gingerly lie down next to him, careful of his leg, and hold his hand while resting her head on his shoulder. Siera came to sit on my lap so I could hold her and reassure her that everyone was fine now. We all stayed there until they fell asleep.

Eventually I carried the girls to their beds, then Tucker to my bed, and asked for more strength while my silent crying commenced. Even now, I can adamantly say that the night of Sunday, November 8, was one of the worst nights of my life.

Chapter Five

The following morning, Mom and Dad were back to help the girls get ready and delivered to school since I had to have Tucker to the hospital by 7:30. Luckily, I was able to give him another dose of the painkillers during the night, so he wasn't in physical discomfort while I moved him and carried him to the car.

Kevin drove so I could sit in the back seat with Tucker. My boy wasn't too afraid of surgery because he knew that both Judd and I had undergone surgeries on our knees for sports injuries. *Damn, how I wish that were all this was.* I kept my positive attitude, talking about how he got to miss school and wondering what we should have for supper that night. I have never had any interest in acting, but I sure did a good job during all this. Inside I knew we were bringing Tucker to surgery to confirm a very rare and horrific cancer. But I also knew I was never going to let my son die. I had to get him through this so all three of my kids could be happy and healthy once again.

We eventually found our way to the right floor and the right room. I distinctly remember taking joy in not being able to find my way through the U of M Masonic Children's Hospital. I told myself to savor that feeling—with treatment lasting a minimum of eight months, I would eventually know the layout of this place as well as I knew the layout of ISLA. Judd and I hung out with Tucker in the pre-op room and learned how that process went. Lots of people came in and out of the room with various questions and preparatory procedures to complete. One attribute of Tucker's that worked well with hospitals was his love of TV and movies. That came in quite handy with all the waiting we had to do that morning and every subsequent visit to the hospital.

Despite Dr. Clohisy clearing his schedule, he and the floor were busy that morning, so we had to wait a couple hours. Periodically, another of Tucker's visitors would stop by. It was nice for him to see Lisa, Kris, her husband Jeff, Grandpa Gary, and Kevin, and Grandma came after getting the girls to school.

It was finally time to bring him to the surgery. I was thrilled that I could stay with Tucker all the way into the operating room; I had to suit up like I was about to walk on the moon, but that provided the opportunity to have my boy laugh at me. Tucker loved that, and I loved to hear his laugh, so it was a win-win. Again, I had the happy smile on my face as I told him how proud I was of him. He was doing such an amazing job being brave.

I held his hand as he was rolled to the operating room—his sweet, soft little hand. The room was big, bright, and white. I got to stay there while they administered the sleeping med. I didn't know how much longer I could keep smiling while inside I was so overwhelmed and sad. Surprisingly, Tucker was asleep within a minute. I stayed another minute, not wanting to leave his side. The nurses could tell; finally, one put her hand on my arm and told me they would take great care of my son, then led me out of the room. I really, really didn't want to leave. I was supposed to be the one to fix my child, or at least hold his hand when someone else did.

It was only because of Dr. Clohisy's demeanor that I could

have a little peace leaving the operating room. He'd already made me feel like he loved Tucker and was going to take excellent care of him. No wonder he and Dr. Koop were friends; they were both put on this earth to heal children while reassuring their parents.

Luckily, I had my support crew there to sit with me: Mom, Lisa, and Sara. Unlike Mom and Lisa, who are both firstborns, Sara is not the person who takes charge of a situation. She is happy to do what is asked of her and does it superbly. Sara is the "Robin" to all us leaders. While she doesn't take on the superhero role, her strength, loyalty, and support are what allow each of us to be stronger and more successful. Often Sara's role is more demanding than "Batman's" roles, because she is the Robin to everyone, often at the same time. Like Lisa and Mom, Sara is extraordinary.

Dr. Clohisy came out a couple hours later and confirmed that it was osteosarcoma. Judd tried one last attempt at denial and asked, "Don't we have to wait for the lab results to be sure?" Dr. Clohisy said he had no doubt. It was osteosarcoma. A very rare bone cancer in this very sweet little boy.

I hurried to go see Tucker in post-op. He was already waking up, and the nurses were offering him popsicles (they had red and orange ones; guess which one Tucker chose). I was happy he wasn't in pain; he was holding Dr. Fuzzball, his newly named stuffed animal from his sisters, right where Kayci wished she could be. I texted Kayci's and Siera's teachers to let them know Tucker was out of surgery and doing great. Best of all, he would be home when they got home from school.

Day one was over. Just eight to ten months to go.

Chapter Six

By Tuesday, Tucker had quickly recovered from the surgery and was ready to go to school right away. He always loved going to school, especially for the socializing. Tucker wanted to play with everyone and made friends easily. He was very popular; he liked everyone, and everyone liked him. In fact, one day in first grade, the morning question on the whiteboard was "What is your favorite privilege at ISLA?" Out of his twenty-four classmates, six of them wrote "To get to play with Tucker." Not only did his forty-five third-grade classmates like him, but also kids of all grades and the entire staff, right down to Scott the Lunch Guy.

This special ability to make friends had been evident by age two. During our Target runs, Tucker would say hi to many people. Often he would insist I push the cart closer to any lady who didn't notice him waving. In restaurants he would ask to go talk to the other customers, especially grandpas. He would just walk over to the table and say hi, then chat until our food came and I had to bring him back. At age three, I started letting Tucker and Kayci play in the McDonald's PlayPlace while I waited for our order. By the time Siera and I brought the food to our booth and called for them to come eat, at least three kids would say, "Tucker, eat quickly and hurry back!" Only five minutes had transpired, and kids already loved playing with him and had learned his name.

For many years I just thought Tucker was social, but what

I learned from those who watched him interact with children was that he made kids feel special. He liked them instantly and assumed they would be fun to play with. No one had to be fast enough or good at sports or meet any other criteria. Tucker saw value and good in everyone he met and therefore asked them to play.

He was also the first to notice if someone was sad and stop what he was doing to attend to that person. The first time this became obvious was in the nursing home on the day my grandma was dying. I was there all day with Tucker and Kayci, as we'd been told this would be the day she would pass. Tucker was just two years old and not fully aware of what was going on, nor did he know my aunts and uncles who were there. I had Kayci on my lap in the visitors' room, and Tucker was standing beside me. He watched my uncle, about seven chairs down. He wasn't crying, but he was quiet, resting his face in his hands. Tucker reached into my bag and got out his animal crackers. Then he walked down to my uncle and asked if he wanted one.

My uncle smiled and said, "Sure." After handing him one, Tucker placed his hand on my uncle's knee and looked into his eyes. Then he said, "You can have the rest of them if you want." Tucker always wanted to make people happy, which is how he made friends instantly.

I made sure to enjoy this week of all four of us being together, at home and at ISLA. I didn't know what the treatment plan would be, but I anticipated a lot of time in the hospital. We would find out soon, and soon the kids would hear the c-word for the first time.

"Soon" came on Monday, November 16, in the Journey Clinic on the ninth floor of the hospital.

While leaving ISLA early with the three kids, I was so sick to my stomach I wanted to throw up. Kayci was even more quiet than usual, Siera was just happy to be with all of us, and Tucker simply watched the movie playing in the car. I'd had many conversations with various hospital staff on the best way to tell the kids; they'd specifically told me which words to avoid and to be optimistic rather than realistic. They were five, seven, and eight, for god's sake—they needed to be given the kid version of the news.

Well, I got my first lesson that I was not always going to be in charge where cancer was involved. Apparently being a school psychologist for twenty years and these children's mother for nearly nine years didn't mean I knew how to approach sharing this news. I was not at all happy with how this meeting went.

The kids and I were met by Judd, Kris, Lisa, Kevin, and my parents. Tucker's social worker, Anne, greeted the group and brought us back into an office to wait for Dr. Brenda Weigel, who was Tucker's lead oncologist. We learned that there is a lot of waiting for doctors; their jobs are beyond demanding, and taking care of cancer patients' families can take a while. So, I sat there and waited for the moment my children would hear the worst news of their lives. The moment they would lose their sense of safety and security. The moment they would face the concept of death, of Tucker's death. The moment their lives would never be easy and carefree again. It was a horrible wait on a horrible day in a horrible place.

The only thing worse than waiting was having it happen. In walked Dr. Weigel, her fellow Dr. Will, Anne, and a child-family-life therapist to help take care of the kids. The latter offered to take Kayci and Siera to the playroom, but they chose to stay. Tucker sat on the mini hospital bed, Kayci and Siera at a little table; I held Tucker's hand, with Judd on the other side of him. When the doctors commented on the crowded room, I let them know there were more who hadn't come but would definitely be around often.

I called Kayci and Siera over to my lap as Dr. Weigel began her speech. I don't remember it exactly, but it did have the c-word in it—often. Dr. Weigel explained that the surgery showed that Tucker had a disease in his leg called osteosarcoma, which was bone cancer. I could feel my children's fear. I couldn't hug them fast enough or hard enough. I so desperately wanted the next sentence to be, *"But we are going to fix that so he is as good as new."* But it was nothing like that.

She went on to explain that there were ways to treat the cancer with chemotherapy, but the chemotherapy was a very strong medicine and would have some bad side effects. *Make her STOP!* I was yelling in my head. *Why do children have to hear all this?* Finally, Siera did a tremendous job of self-advocating and asked if she could go see the playroom. I encouraged Kayci to go with her, but she would not leave—she was going to stay there with her brother. *I* wanted to go to the toy room; I don't know how Kayci had the strength not to.

Instead, she stayed there, listening to the horrible news and information. We learned that the chemo treatments would ruin Tucker's fertility, and he was too young to harvest any sperm. *I just found out my son will never have biological children. Can we stop now?* No. The doctor went on to explain other side effects of the poison they would be pumping into my son. It would age his heart—with every round of chemo, his heart would get a little older. When he was forty, he would have the heart of a fifty-year-old or older. Dr. Weigel went on with another horrible tidbit: he would lose some of his hearing, but hopefully not in the speaking ranges. He would also lose his hair.

She wrapped up with the great news that *if* everything went well and his tumor responded to chemotherapy, this could take as little as nine to ten months. All his treatments had to be inpatient. I asked for the definition of that word, hoping my guess wasn't right, only to be told that all the treatment had to be administered in the hospital. *Damnit, I was right.* Tucker would be checking into the hospital on Mondays and ideally released on Thursdays. Plus, he would need blood draws twice every week as well as periodic heart and hearing tests and scans. Those damn scans.

Overall, they told us he would be in the hospital about fifteen days a month for the next three months. Then, he would have surgery to remove the cancerous portion of his femur. After that, another six to seven months of chemo.

Finally, Dr. Weigel stopped and asked if there were any questions. Kayci, still sitting on my lap while holding Tucker's hand, had a question—one I can't even repeat without crying. Dr. Weigel looked at her and asked, "What's your question, sweetheart?"

Kayci responded, "Is my brother going to die?"

See?! I knew this was going to be the end of their childhood innocence! My daughter should be thinking about what snack she wants, not if her brother, her best friend, her lifelong roommate is going to die! I hate you, cancer!

And when Dr. Weigel answered, I hated her! My mother-reflex blurted out the words, "Of course not!" But she didn't allow my response to be the final one. She answered, "That is what everyone in this room is trying to prevent. We are all going to work really hard to take the best care of your brother."

I was so mad! *How does that reassure a little seven-year-old? Or a forty-six-year-old mother, for that matter?* I decided that, after this, I was going to be the one giving the updates to my children.

Kayci isn't easy to understand in many ways, but one thing was obvious: she idolized her big brother. From the instant she and I had come home from her birth, Tucker had doted on her, always caressing her cheek and kissing her forehead. He was only fifteen months old when she was born, but he had the nature of a sweet little old grandma. Since the time Kayci could walk, Tucker had brought her everywhere he went, literally—he would take her by the wrist and say, "Come on, let's go play in our room." He loved to help her crawl into his crib so they could bounce around together. Then he would crawl out, get her binky and some books, and crawl back in to read to her. They were never apart, and Kayci loved every. Single. Minute.

Luckily, she loved sports just like Tucker, because he insisted I sign her up for T-ball with him even though she was younger than the age cutoff. I had to get special permission, but it worked out well; Kayci hit the ball better than all the other kids, except her big brother, and always listened to the coach. Thus it began that they would always be on the same teams. Other than also being a great athlete, Kayci was the opposite of Tucker. She was quiet and shy. She studied every situation before ever inserting herself into it. With Tucker, however, she never had to enter anything alone, not daycare, preschool, a party, or even a room. He was always by her side.

And now Kayci had just heard she might not have him by her side ever again. *How can this be happening?*

To cope with all this information, Tucker lay back on the bed while I rubbed his head and Kayci and Judd held his hands. Ten minutes into the talk, Tucker had his eyes shut, which I am sure was partly so he wouldn't see the pain in Kayci's eyes, so he could try to shut everything out. Besides, he didn't have to hear any of this; soon enough, he would be living it, and some side effects he would be living with for the rest of his life.

It was a long drive home. Mom and Dad came over and picked up some food for dinner, but I can't remember what we ate or did. I didn't even know how to care for any of my three kids. I was in shock, devastated. Thankfully, I was not alone. Sara brought her children Mason and Paige over, and there was a Wild game to watch. That's Sara—not on the front lines, but running to care for everyone who is. The noise and game provided the distraction we needed, and the family provided the support.

Tucker and I would be back at the hospital in the morning to start the tests. Then chemo would start on Thursday. Childhood was ending for a time, at least nine months. The nightmare that had started for me twelve days ago was now Tucker's, Kayci's, and Siera's nightmare too.

Chapter Seven

Typically, I like to confront things head-on and never worry about doing too much, so no one was surprised that I decided to get all Tucker's medical appointments taken care of in one day. That way, he could have a full day at school on Wednesday, before starting chemotherapy on Thursday. *Wow, Thursday.* In forty-eight hours, my son would be a full-blown cancer patient, locked in a hospital with poison dripping into his little body. The only pro (I still have a hard time using the word "good" in any sentence concerning cancer) was that there was so much to do and so much to learn that my brain had to focus on one hour at a time.

Tuesday morning, I got Kayci and Siera ready and then dropped them off at school, the whole time reassuring them that Tucker would be fine today. I explained that he was just getting lots of things like X-rays, nothing that would hurt him. Then I talked about their day in an attempt to make them feel equally important. I parked and walked them in, knowing that soon this would no longer be part of our routine. Nor would bringing them home, spending the evening with them, or tucking them into bed. Cancer is so cruel to the entire family.

I hurried back home to finish getting Tucker ready, carried him out to the car, and got to the hospital by 10:00 a.m. He needed an IV placed and a blood draw. Tucker is terrified of needles, but the lidocaine helped. That was his first "poke," as they call it in the pediatric cancer world. He then got a CT scan of his chest and a full-body bone scan. Luckily, I could stay in the room by his side for the entire bone scan as he slowly, so slowly, went through the tube. I did have to step out of the room for one scan, and it physically hurt me to let go of his hand. It was over quickly, however, so I hurried back into the room.

Next there was an ultrasound of his very healthy heart, the heart that would never be that healthy again, then a very long wheelchair ride through the underground tunnels of the hospital over to the clinic for his extensive hearing test. At least that one didn't feel so "medical" and was a nice distraction for Tucker. I was still angry that in order for a child to be treated for cancer, his body had to be damaged permanently. I couldn't even bring myself to touch the thought of Tucker as a young adult having to tell his girlfriend that perhaps she wouldn't want to marry him because he could never give her biological children.

It had been a very long day by the time we were finally done, around five o'clock. I had made the rookie mistake of thinking we would have idle time and bringing my work laptop; instead, I'd had to lift Tucker in and out of his wheelchair about fifteen times while also carrying our coats and bags around the hospital all day. I was still a full-time special education teacher; I had students who needed my help and paperwork to be done within very demanding and legally enforced timelines. However, I was not able to focus on anything but my child, so I learned to never bring work to appointment days again.

My back was sore, but I was just glad that Tucker now had effective pain relief so he wouldn't yell or even grimace each time I picked him up and put him down. I couldn't believe my super-athlete son hadn't been able to walk for eighteen days. He no longer argued about the wheelchair, nor did he ask to take the immobilizer off. His leg hurt if it was even slightly bent.

Tucker held up well throughout the day. It was helpful to have a child-family-life (CFL) therapist there to explain the procedures for each test and offer distraction in the form of iPad activities. When we finally got home, the girls were thrilled to see us. Not nearly as much as I was to see them.

While the kids were relaxing after dinner, I got to work on the emotional task of going public. I knew I would be creating a page for Tucker on the CaringBridge website, where caretakers can keep family and friends updated on the medical conditions of their loved ones. I hadn't started the journal yet, partly because there wasn't time but mostly because of my plan to keep all the bad news a secret from the kids for as long as possible. But Tucker would only have one day in school, so I needed to let parents know. It wasn't just my three children that would be profoundly affected by this. So many eight-year-olds were about to witness cancer close-up and see a friend be very different from them, from how he was before. This was nothing to overlook or minimize. These kids needed support too, and all that had to start with information so they could start to process it. So, I sent this email out to all the ISLA parents:

Dear ISLA Families and Friends,

Today I reach out to you to share some news not as an ISLA teacher, but as an ISLA mom. Two weeks ago, I found out my son Tucker, who is in third grade, has bone cancer. What started as a sore leg from what we thought was an accident on a slide was then considered a fracture, then ultimately ended up being osteosarcoma, a cancerous tumor in his femur.

Luckily, after the devastating news, we received the good news that we caught it early! And although very rare (only 600 children a year in the US get this diagnosis), it is very treatable! We have done nearly all of the preliminary tests and appointments, and Tucker will begin chemotherapy on Thursday. [After] ten months of chemo and a surgery to remove the tumorous bone in a few months, we should be looking back at this difficult ordeal. By next fall, Tucker will be back on the baseball field and hockey rink as a healthy, happy fourth grader.

I share this so that you as parents have the opportunity to tell your children tonight. My children—Tucker, Kayci, who is in second grade, and Siera, who is in kindergarten—all found out yesterday. The girls will be missing their brother while he spends a considerable amount of time in the hospital. However, I know they will be supported while at ISLA by our amazing community and at home by their amazing extended family.

For those of you who wish to discuss this with your child(ren), here is a great, concise resource to help you:

Tucker and I will be at school tomorrow and will answer any questions his classmates or Kayci's classmates have about this. I will have a CaringBridge site in place for Tucker in the next day or two if you are interested in following our journey as we beat this thing.

Thank you for your time; and thank you in advance for the kindness I know you and your children will show me and my children. ISLA is a tremendous community, and if my kids and I have to go through this, I can't imagine a better school community to be in during this time.

Very sincerely,

Dana, Tucker, Kayci, Siera, and Tucker's dad, Judd

I truly did not want these children to be terrified and was determined to keep everyone positive. By showing determination and not fear, I believed that the children, including mine, would be able to be optimistic and even forget about the hellish journey on which we found ourselves.

On Wednesday, while it wasn't easy, Tucker went to school for the full day. He had a lot of anxiety about being in his wheelchair, being tired, being different, and being in pain. Along with his leg, Tucker was also sore above the brace in his groin and below the brace in front of his ankle. I figured out that with his stress, he must be always flexing these muscles, so the poor guy had worn out the few muscles that were still available to him on his right leg.

I gave Kayci's class of second graders a quick presentation about what she would be going through and what disease her brother had. It was a good discussion, and her teacher, who had also been Tucker's second-grade teacher, was extra helpful. I believed it was important for classmates to understand that Kayci would be acting differently sometimes so they could be supportive. Afterall, whether at her dad's house or ours, Kayci had only spent two nights without Tucker beside her. This was going to change drastically, and the reason they would be separated couldn't have been more different than Tucker's two sleepovers with friends.

Next, I presented to Tucker's class. Normally he didn't mind being the center of attention, so it saddened me to see him choosing to stay in the back of his class, looking embarrassed and scared. I started to describe cancer as "bad cells." When I was asked what a "cell" is, I found a way to put it in terms a third grader could understand: Legos. I explained that cells are like 1x1 Lego units; individually they're very small, but when stacked together they make very big structures. I told them to think of a body made up of 1x1 Legos. I went on to explain that Legos are supposed to be a variety of bright colors: red, blue, yellow, green, and in Tucker's case, orange. It was cute that the kids finished that sentence before I could.

"Well, cancer cells are black 1x1s, and they can take over the healthy, colorful 1x1 pieces in a person's body," I continued. "In Tucker's case, the 1x1s in his right thigh bone now have some black Legos. Right now, there are just a few, but they are expanding and trying to ruin more colorful, healthy ones and replace them with more black ones. Therefore, Tucker needs to go into the hospital to get a type of medicine, called chemotherapy, that kills black Legos so they don't get to keep adding more 1x1s."

The classmates asked a lot of questions about the "black Legos": How do Legos start turning black? Could they get black Legos too? How many 1x1s did Tucker have now? I was glad we were talking in terms of Legos (although it meant I had to check on registered copyright laws before publishing this book). It was so much better than the c-word. In the fifteen-minute discussion, the word "cancer" would have been stated over a couple dozen times, and no adult, let alone a kid, needs to hear that word that often.

As I answered questions about chemotherapy, Tucker spoke up from the back of the room, declaring we weren't going to use that word either. I was a little surprised but loved that he was going to take control of the narrative. He couldn't control the cancer inside his body, but he could control the conversations about it.

Tucker said we were going to call the chemo "T." I asked for clarification: "Do you mean like hot tea? The drink?" Tucker said no, just "T." It was adopted not only by his classmates and our family, but all the doctors and nurses as well after I explained it to them. When anyone, including the hospital staff, would say the word "chemo" around us, Tucker and I were sure to correct them. I have to admit, having doctors with twenty years of experience working with cancer and chemotherapy using the terms "black Legos" and "T" to honor my son's wishes was pretty cool.

We then went on to introduce "Curious George" to the class. There is an adorable program called "There's a Monkey in My Chair" we learned about through Tucker's oncology social worker. Tucker received a stuffed monkey, about three feet long, who came complete with his own backpack. Tucker named this guy "Curious George" after his first and all-time-favorite children's show, which I loved. He and I would watch "Monkey" every morning as he sat in his personalized toddler chair and I sat next to him on the floor, leaning back against the couch and sharing a Pop-Tart. I always wanted to be right next to my kids.

The Monkey in My Chair program had Tucker's classmates physically put "George" in Tucker's desk chair on the days he was not in school because of the cancer—I mean black Legos. George didn't just fill Tucker's chair; he participated in the class and even collected homework that came home in his backpack. Kayci liked having the job of backpack courier. It was so wonderful how Tucker's teacher, Señora Shrestha, got George so involved. George even cheated on the spelling test—Señora Shrestha found him with the answer book right on his lap! He also went to art and music classes, and loved being part of phys ed class. Tucker's least favorite part was how well George and

Kayci brought home all the schoolwork he needed to do, but it was worth it to get the stories and see the pictures of George's antics for the day.

I wish this day had ended with the fun of introducing Curious George, but hardly ever is there a day of fun during a child's war with cancer without a body blow of bad news or physical or mental pain. By the end of the school day, Tucker's ankle was in a lot of pain. When he asked if there could be more black Legos in his ankle, I automatically responded, "Of course not, honey!" I found it so easy to lie when I needed to reassure my children that Tucker was going to be OK. In reality, I was terrified it was more cancer; that his leg would need to be amputated; that cancer had already spread. But I stayed calm and cavalier as we hurried home to get some more oxycodone for that pain.

As I pulled up in front of the house, my phone rang. I answered it, but in hindsight I shouldn't have. The kids were tired and distraught, and Tucker was actually yelling in pain from the backseat of the van. I thought the call was about tomorrow's admittance into the hospital, but it wasn't. Dr. Will, the fellow working with Dr. Weigel, had called to tell me about Tucker's scan results.

Every muscle in my body tensed except my face, which fought to keep the same calm expression. I was terrified to hear about the bone scan—maybe there were more tumors?

Dr. Will started with the good news that Tucker's bone scan was "clean." I should have stopped there, but I got greedy hoping for more good news and told him to continue with the other reports. That was a mistake.

The CT scan was not good. Dr. Will told me that there had been "several nodules" found on Tucker's lungs. Hearing my first scan result, while driving, with kids screaming, I don't know why I didn't just hang up. Most likely *because* it was my first scan result, and I did not realize those turn out to be like finding out whether your child will live or die—whether cancer will execute or allow life to continue.

We'd arrived in front of the house, and the kids wanted to get out. Tucker was still yelling—I needed to get him unloaded, which would be so much more painful since the oxy had worn off. I also needed to get the girls away from those already too familiar screams. But I was stuck there, listening to the doctor say, "This will make things much more difficult."

As the kids were with me, I did my best to speak in code and asked why the treatment wouldn't "rectify" this situation. *Seriously, eight months of chemotherapy that requires him to be in the hospital fifteen days a month can't take care of "several nodules"?*

Dr. Will said, "There is a chance it could, but most likely not." *Really? Why haven't I hung up? Or thrown my phone into the street?* He went on to say that Tucker would now most likely need surgery on his lungs after these ten months of treatment. How appropriate that Tucker was screaming in the background; it provided the soundtrack for what was happening inside my brain and entire body.

I can't really say I recovered from that news; there was no time to let if fully sink in. The girls both had gymnastics and there was no way I was going to ruin even a minute of normalcy to let horrible news penetrate. I gave Tucker his pain medication, fed the kids, invited Jayden over to play with and distract Tucker, and then asked Kevin to stay with them. I brought the girls to gymnastics and then out for a DQ treat. Of course, we brought one home for Tucker. His favorite was the red Star Kiss, only because they didn't have orange.

That night, I racked my brain to think of everything that would be good for my and Tucker's hospital stay and what to prep for the girls for the next two days of school. Being busy and having to think through details was helpful. I always preferred to think rather than feel the fear of our new reality.

As I set out two nice outfits for the girls, I got very sad that Tucker wouldn't need one. On Saturday, he and I would be in the hospital while my parents hosted a larger-than-normal Thanksgiving feast for my mom's extended family. It had been planned for six weeks and involved over twenty-five cousins and second cousins joining the A-Team for a meal with all the trimmings. Many encouraged me to attend and leave Tucker at the hospital with Judd, but I couldn't imagine leaving him behind. But I also couldn't imagine Kayci and Siera at a huge family celebration without me or Tucker. Nor could I imagine not seeing them for all four days of inpatient. For that matter, I still couldn't believe any of this was happening.

I got very little sleep that night, but I remember thinking that I would be able to catch up on sleep in the hospital. I thought Tucker would be sleeping a lot, that I would be able to rest, sleep, and catch up on paperwork.

I was wrong. So wrong.

Chapter Eight

Thursday morning, Judd came to our house to take the girls to breakfast. It helped distract them and gave Judd a little alone time with them. I had Tucker watching his favorite morning shows, which many times included the recording of the third period of the Wild game if they'd played the night before. When the girls returned, I took them to the doctor for their flu vaccinations to make sure they could always be around their brother. Eventually, I got them to ISLA and walked them to their classrooms. With a smile on my face and my "everything is going to be fine" attitude, I gave them a hug and told them to call me after school. Inside, my heart was hurting for these girls—just five and seven, and they had so much to worry about.

As I was leaving Kayci's classroom, Tucker's teacher asked me to come into her room and said the students had something for him. One of his buddies had bought a white-collared shirt and made a stand for it out of cardboard. He'd brought it to school that morning for all the other third graders to sign for Tucker. They wanted him to wear it before his surgery today to have all of them "with" him. Their messages of love and encouragement were beyond heartwarming. It was amazing how they jumped into action so quickly to support their friend.

I brought it home, and Tucker put it on right away. Then Tucker, Judd, Kevin, and I drove to the hospital for his one o'clock appointment to get admitted, have his port put in, and then possibly start the "T." *Here we go. Let's get this started so we can get rid of this [bleep] cancer and get this boy healthy.*

We checked in and got our page of Tucker-labels, which we were to carry with us to all our appointments so various staff could stick them to whatever lab sample they collected. We were then sent to the surgical floor to "place his port." I was surprised that to "place" actually meant to wheel him into an operating room, put him under, slice open his upper chest beneath his shoulder, and put a disc-shaped thing under his skin. We were in a pre-op room learning about this as it was about to happen. This was not how Tucker liked to approach things. He preferred time to process and mentally prepare. The CFL therapist and I worked to keep his anxiety at bay—luckily, Tucker loves movies and they are a great distraction.

Once again, I walked my little boy into an operating room; this one was much smaller, so I can see why this procedure had different terminology. Tucker was back in less than an hour, just enough time for me to have yet another large Diet Coke to manage my stress and exhaustion. His "port" was in and already "accessed."

Oh, how I miss the days when I had no idea what these words were. I hate that I, and so many parents, now speak fluent "cancer." "Accessing" was when the nurse pushed two different needles through Tucker's skin into the rubber center of the port. The needles were connected to tiny tubes for an IV to go right into Tucker's chest. This allowed the nurses to get IV access without having to find a vein and put it in his arm. All Tucker's T (chemo), fluids, and IV medicines went through his port for the duration of his treatment.

Next, we wheeled up to the fifth floor and checked into Tucker's "apartment." Once again, Tucker applied his own names to things that were less scary, which I think is an excellent way to manage the anxiety of a terrifying situation. The nurses loved his name for his hospital room, and I have to agree it was very much like an apartment. With a little imagination, it had three bedrooms, a kitchenette, and a three-quarter bath. Judd took the couch, which was his bedroom; I had the recliner for my bedroom; and Tucker had the master bedroom, which was the hospital bed. Tucker's favorite "room" was the living room (very close to all three bedrooms), which had a huge screen TV run by the control panel attached to his bed. There was even mood lighting and message boards Tucker could control.

I started to unpack. First Tucker's clothes—after that stay, I learned he would need hardly anything other than pajama pants. He, like the other kids, pretty much stayed shirtless and in the same pair of shorts. Then I unpacked mine. Turned out I didn't need many either, due to not having much time or energy to bother dressing and undressing. But it was nice to have a little closet full of orange clothes.

I next set up the kitchenette: a six-pack of Diet Coke and a six-pack of Diet Mountain Dew for me, some SunnyD for Tucker, and Dum Dums suckers for all the guests. It turned out I had underpacked food; eventually I was bringing lots more of Tucker's favorite things, hoping he would eat, and lots more treats for guests, nurses, and nurses' aides. I left my shampoo and other toiletries zipped up in my bag and placed that in the closet. It was pretty much in the same state when I packed to go home, as there was neither time nor motivation to primp or even shower.

Like I said earlier, I made the rookie mistake of expecting a long weekend to physically relax, catch up on sleep, and hold Tucker's hand. It had been ten days since Tucker's biopsy. Carrying, lifting, and moving him, taking a couple trips to the bathroom each night, and massaging his ankle and groin muscles hourly around the clock left me physically exhausted. I was excited to have help during the night so I could sleep. That thought could not have been further from the reality that awaited me. These "fluids" that they started giving Tucker right when we got to the apartment were continuous. And all fluids that go in, must come out.

The process started with several hours of fluids to get Tucker's body ready to receive the T. It was so poisonous that the body had to have higher concentrations of fluids in before the "medicine" gets administered. Then the body had to be flushed out after it was administered. This T was so toxic that we all had to wear gloves to even handle the urinal bottle and a face mask when pouring it into the toilet. Think of that. It was so dangerous that even a splash after being peed out could make a person sick, yet it was being poured directly into a seventy-pound boy and circulating through his little body.

I had always wanted a son, for so many reasons. That first night in the hospital added one more reason to the very long list: boys can pee into a urinal bottle, and with very little movement needed. However, I, the transporter of urine, did have to be awake, get gloves on, and not move my son's pained leg, all without turning on too many lights to wake him up, yet making sure the aim was good so there were no spills. Spills meant a lot of movement would be required, for Tucker, me, and the nursing staff. That wasn't good. The few times that happened, there were tears and angry words from the sweet little boy who was very mad to be sitting in urine.

Oh, those were very long nights. And given my boy's desire for privacy, very long days, since he would only allow me or his dad to help him. I was too tired then to do the math, but now I can calculate it was about thirty times I transported urine in the bottle over to the bathroom. It was incredibly exhausting.

Friday morning, the T started. By that time, I was very excited—it had been over two weeks that I knew Tucker had cancer growing inside him, and he had been in tremendous pain for so long. The oxycodone helped, but it wore off every four hours, and the ten minutes until the new dose kicked in were so hard for Tucker and so miserable for me to hear. The osteosarcoma cells were multiplying and taking up more room in his leg, thus forcing more pressure on everything inside. Procedurally, it was easy to start the T—it was just a different bag of fluid hung on his medicine pole. However, it was obvious when it was T because the nurses would come in wearing protective gear just short of a hazmat suit. Also, there were a lot of buttons to push on the med boxes hanging on the IV pole to control the flow of the poison going into the child. But that was what would kill the black Legos, and we needed those to be gone.

Within a couple hours, the T was working. Well, I chose that conclusion for my own mental well-being. Tucker had been battling the pain throughout the night; he even needed morphine. But after the T started, his pain scale number was reduced by half. By the afternoon it was down to one-fourth. I made Tucker calculate the fractions—don't forget the teacher in me is always looking for teachable moments. It took forty-eight hours to administer the two bags of T, because it was so potent it had to drip into Tucker at the rate of one ounce per hour. There were also two other types of chemotherapy which were given simultaneously.

Along with Tucker's pain relief, there was more "good" news on this day. One of the veteran oncologists met with us to discuss the results of those horrible chest CT scan results. Lisa left work to come listen with me and Judd, and Papa came to hang out with Tucker, as I never left him alone in his hospital room.

It turned out that Dr. Will's explanation had been harsher than it needed to be. Thirty years of experience does make a difference. We were relieved to have Dr. Neglia explain the lung nodules in a much less alarming way, though the news was still very, very disheartening. Yes, the fact that the cancer had metastasized to Tucker's lungs was not good, but there were only a couple "spots" (a much less daunting word than nodule) and they were "tiny." Then Dr. Neglia added examples of a person with many more spots who had gone on to beat osteosarcoma. *Please let that be Tucker's story.*

Tucker had a few little ones (approximately two millimeters in size), four medium ones (four millimeters), and two larger ones (five millimeters). We didn't know which ones were or were not cancerous; most likely the big ones were. The bad news was that this meant the cancer had spread from its original source, which, yes, added more steps to the process. However, Dr. Neglia didn't make it sound like it would be "more difficult" in terms of figuring out what to do. We would still go through the first nine to ten months as planned. There was reason to hope that the T would at least reduce all the nodules if not eliminate them altogether. However, even if that happened, Tucker would need to have surgery after all the chemo to remove all the nodules and have them tested. Hopefully each one would be a dead little dried-up piece of stupid cancer.

Osteosarcoma is known for showing up in the lungs after you think it is gone. That is why there is so much T and why it is so strong. If there were any signs of cancer life in the nodules at that point, then they would have to figure out what to give Tucker next. The good news was that all the nodules were in locations that would be easy to extract. *What a huge relief. We can get them out, if they don't die before then.* Should that be the case, we would know better what to do from the results of a study that was underway regarding exactly that situation. And Dr. Weigel was the head of the study. (I was less mad at her now.)

So, I chose to compartmentalize this concern, along with 90 percent of the other things I could have worried or thought about. I needed to live one day at a time. I was thankful for the little progress we made each day, like that day's improvement on Tucker's pain. I knew we would beat this.

Friday evening, Judd decided to go home. I was both surprised and relieved. Surprised because for a week we had been arguing about who would be staying with Tucker and where the girls would be staying. I'd insisted that I would be in the hospital beside Tucker every single night and for every appointment, just as it had been with each doctor and dentist appointment and the three trips to the ER during our children's lives. Judd had told me I had to leave half the nights so he could be there. I can't even come up with a metaphor for how implausible that was. However, once Judd realized how uncomfortable the couch was and how many interruptions there would be, he reconsidered his plan to spend nights in the hospital.

Throughout the journey, I was angered many times by Judd's

choices to step back and let all the work fall on me. Starting with that first night, I was the one helping Tucker pee in the urinal bottle every time. I remember wondering why a dad wouldn't be invested in these "boy" duties. In our family, I always stepped up, which allowed Judd to stay on the bench.

Now, after much introspection and time passed, I see that both my and Judd's natures created this norm. I am incapable of not being in charge of my children, and I have the inner strength and outer support to withstand all the demands required to do so. Judd enjoys the fun tasks of parenting and is very comfortable with handing off the difficult tasks, especially the emotionally difficult ones.

I wish I would have had this insight during that war. I had so much added pain from worrying that Tucker was being hurt by his father's spotty attendance, his statements about needing to leave to avoid traffic, his not making a Perkins run because it would be another parking ramp fee. There were many arguments between me and Judd about where donations would go, where the girls would stay, him coming to visit, and so much more. Like we often did, we made even the worst situation worse—me with my determination that I knew what was best for our children, and Judd with his angry and hurtful verbal responses to this even as his physical actions showed that he was very willing to have it be that way.

However, today I am grateful for our roles in this war. I was on the front line with Tucker in battle, always looking back at Kayci and Siera, making the calls regarding their care and wellbeing. Judd was a soldier in the guard, providing hospital visits for distraction and fun, caring for the girls over school breaks if

Tucker and I were in the hospital, and giving excellent support and care when Tucker was at his house.

Thankfully I didn't need personal support from Judd; I had that from my family, and there was an honorary member of the A-Team who will forever be family. I met Dayra de la Cruz when I started working at ISLA, and was thrilled to have her as Tucker's first-grade teacher. Dayra loves her students as if they were her own children, and their parents love her. Upon learning of Tucker's diagnosis, she insisted that she move into our home so she could do all the housekeeping and childcare I couldn't get accomplished. She told me that my job was to take care of Tucker full-time, and Kayci and Siera when I could, and she would take care of the rest. I considered telling her she didn't have to, but I knew she wouldn't take no for an answer, so I welcomed her support. Plus, I knew she needed to be helping as much as I needed the help. It is who she is. With her efforts at home, some of the burden was eased, and my children were never anything less than cared for. Family or not, we were blessed with so many helpers.

Chapter Nine

Saturday presented a new painful choice. The extended family Thanksgiving was happening at my parents' house, where my healthy daughters would be. My son was in the hospital with cancer, hooked up to an IV pole. What does a mother choose? Both choices would hurt the children. And either choice would hurt my heart. Judd was back at the hospital, so Tucker wouldn't be alone, but why should I get to go to a party when he couldn't? Tucker's favorite thing was family parties. He loved his cousins like siblings and loved his siblings as much as he loved his parents. *Why should he be the only one who has to miss out? I should have to miss out too.*

But why should Siera and Kayci not get to see their mom? Why should they be the only children at the party without their family beside them? They were already missing their brother, and because of divorce, they were the only cousins without both parents there. *Should they have one parent there? Should I prove to them I love them just as much as I love Tucker, since they hear those words but don't see the fairness? How am I going to make these choices for the next ten months?*

Since it was the girls' first night without me, I finally decided to leave the hospital and go to my parents' house, which was only fifteen minutes away. The drive was hell; sobbing, I considered turning around. I felt like I was abandoning my sick child. This was also my first time being alone in many days. In fact, it was my first time alone since the horrible report on the scans; since Tucker and the girls learning about the cancer; since Tucker was admitted into the hospital; since the words of the phone call twenty-five days ago became reality; since my life and the lives of my children had taken a bullet. I had to make sure all four of us survived that wound. As all that flooded through me, the tears poured out. I didn't think I would ever stop crying.

But then I pulled up to my parents' house and had to. My eyes were like a faucet I could turn off. My brain had a mute switch that I could activate when around children. I forced a smile onto my face and walked into the house to show my daughters that there was nothing to worry about. Tucker was doing great and enjoying the big TV in his room! He liked playing with his hospital bed and had really nice nurses and doctors! The T was working and getting rid of those black Legos! All just happy smiles and great news! Right? As far as my daughters and the four other little cousins were concerned, that was exactly right.

The rest of my family heard the true medical reports and some of my pain, but I still hid much of it. My entire career came from my desire to rid children and parents of pain. In my first job interviews, I told principals that I "fix kids." I am driven to seek what is broken, fix it, and make everyone happy. My family was already suffering from what was happening to their nephew/cousin/grandson; I was not going to add more unhappiness to their lives and hurt myself even further. Instead, I would absorb Tucker's pain and use every skill and ounce of energy I had to lessen it. No one would know how scared and miserable he was, because I would make sure I relieved him of that.

When he said he couldn't, I would tell him he could. When he said it hurt, I would find a way to make it feel better. When he cried, I would wipe his tears. When he asked, *But what if I can't do that?* I would reassure him, *There is nothing we can't do.* This was my plan, and I was going to make it happen. I was not just going to say *There is nothing we can't do*—I was going to believe it fully and overcome every challenge thrown at us. It started as a promise to my son, and then it became our motto.

I didn't stay long at the Thanksgiving party, but I was glad I went; the girls were reassured that everything was good at the hospital and gave me big hugs, which filled me with joy. Siera stayed by me during the meal; when she finished first, she even sat in my lap for a little while. As close as Kayci was to Tucker, that is how close Siera was to me. My mom always jokes about how Siera was on my hip the entire first year of her life. It is true, I held her constantly—I had to for her own safety! Tucker and Kayci were always running around, so I didn't want to lay her on the floor. Also, Kayci was a little jealous, so if Siera was in a bouncy chair or swing, Kayci made sure to give it extra bounce and extra swing.

When Siera was two, Kayci and Tucker already had sport and school events, so she was with me cheering them on. When hockey started, Siera and I spent three hours in the rink watching her siblings every Saturday and Sunday throughout the winter. Well, I watched—Siera dressed her dolls, colored, and learned how to play on my phone. Yes, she was my sidekick.

Tucker loved his little sister immensely and showed that by always asking her about her interests. "What outfit is your doll going to wear today?" "Siera, I love your bracelets!" "What shoes do you like best?" He also liked to teach her things like how to make cupcakes, how to finger paint, and how to play baseball. Kayci was Tucker's best friend, and Siera was his baby sister. When Siera started gymnastics at age two, Kayci had complained that she had to go with, but Tucker never did. He'd liked watching her flip, climb, and swing, and still did. Tucker went to all of Siera's T-ball games and many of her gymnastics practices, always cheering on his little sister. He was a very proud and loving big brother to both his sisters.

When I finished eating the delicious Thanksgiving meal, both Kayci and Siera were busy playing with their cousins. I was reassured that the A-Team had this. They could give just as much love to Kayci and Siera as I could, so I went back to where I was needed most: by Tucker's side.

I'd received the answer to my dilemma. A sick child needs his mother more than the healthy children; however, the healthy children still need her too. This is one of the hardest demands of parenting a child who's battling a life-threatening disease. Over the next several months, I would continually search for ways to invest time and energy into Kayci and Siera, but I knew it would never be as much as I would be spending with Tucker. It is a horrible reality, one that makes healthy children victims just as much as their sick sibling. Thank goodness I had the A-Team, Kevin, and ISLA to help with my daughters. Siera and Kayci suffered much less because of their love, actions, and support.

That night, after Tucker was asleep and I was flipping the sofa into my "bed," I suddenly remembered where I was supposed to be sleeping that night. In October, Kevin had booked a fancy hotel room for the weekend. It was going to be the day he proposed to me and we could officially start the countdown until we were a family of five. He had also reserved plane tickets over Christmas break so Tucker, Kayci, and Siera could meet their future cousins, who lived in Kevin's hometown of Clearwater, Florida. After the diagnosis, Kevin had canceled the hotel room and kept the ring in the box. He also canceled the trip, per Dr. Weigel's instructions. Since he'd bought travel insurance, the tickets were refunded, and we could make the trip once Tucker was better.

Rather than the sparkle of light from a diamond inside a ring box, I fell asleep with the glow of the lights on the boxes on Tucker's IV pole. Cancer ruins everything.

Chapter Ten

Tucker's ninth birthday was November 30, the following Monday. Using my new motto, "There's nothing we can't do," I was determined to make this birthday just as fun as the other eight, despite being far more tired than ever before. Tucker was still waking up five times during the night—well, my "night," which was about 1:00 a.m. to 7:30 a.m. All these trips carrying him back and forth to the bathroom was causing me a lot of back pain.

All of that was ignored, however, and we began Tucker's birthday morning how we start all birthday mornings in this family: with ice cream for breakfast! Complete with candles and singing. For Tucker it was orange sherbet, of course. The girls and I carried the orange bowl into my bed and woke Tucker up with our lovely singing voices (not). Tucker only took a few bites, but I focused more on his beautiful smile and the little sparkle in his eyes as his sisters sat beside him in the bed. Tucker couldn't go to school because his white blood cell count was down to 1.6 the previous Friday. It should be between 5 and 14. This was day five after chemo so his doctors were expecting this dip. Grandma came over to take care of Tucker while the girls and I headed to school.

While Papa does all the evening and weekend babysitting, Grandma does all daytime needs, which works out great because when my children aren't feeling well there is no one I would rather have in charge. She doesn't do the sweet old lady, high-pitched-voice doting. Her style is much more covert. My mom was the first born to a 100 percent Polish farmer and a proud Norwegian farmer's wife. She was out in the fields alongside her dad, driving the tractors and feeding the farm animals. Mom is the perfect combination of her dad's strength, hard work, and a bit of his stubbornness, mixed with her mom's gifts of taking care of everyone's needs and wants, and always going the extra mile for everyone. She loves sports more than any woman of her generation and has taught me everything I know about planning events and using humor and aloofness to deflect fear. Mom is the A-Team matriarch. The creator of all the love, connection, and devotion among and between us. My dad told me he fell in love with her not only for who she was, but also for the mother she would become. He was spot on.

I left work in the afternoon to come home and take Tucker in for his blood draw. Since I was able to arrange for these to happen at our pediatrician's office, it was easy for me to take him and not miss too much work. For each finger poke, Tucker told the nurse which finger to use; apparently his fingertip stayed sore for a while, and he wanted to switch up which one hurt. There isn't much left to control once cancer takes over, so I welcomed and supported when Tucker found some way to have his say in a situation.

Unfortunately, Tucker's white blood cell count had dipped. We discussed whether this meant he would need a blood transfusion, but the doctors listened to my request to wait and see if the cells would recover. I did not want to bring my son to the hospital on his birthday. I understood cancer was doing its thing, but Tucker's mental health was not only important, but necessary to have the best chance to fight this.

When we got home, I gave Tucker his meds. He took them well, but then he threw up. With a call to the doctor, I found out that if you throw up within a half hour of taking medicine, it wasn't absorbed and the whole dose has to be repeated. Taking meds was already a trigger for Tucker's anxiety, and he hated throwing up. Ugh—I knew it would be a very big problem to give them a second time, so I decided to wait a while, hoping that would help.

Papa and Kevin came over for supper. The seven of us enjoyed a great meal left for us by wonderful families who supplied us food through the Meal Train. Tucker ate a ton, which was a present for me. Then he enjoyed playing on the new iPhone that Kevin had given him. Eventually, we had some cupcakes and all sang "Happy Birthday" once again.

Then it was time for me to give Tucker his meds. Tucker could not ease his anxiety, so he panicked and refused to take them. He was crying and yelling, and though I don't want to admit it, after an hour so was I. My dad had to take the girls out of the house again as I shouted things like, "This isn't a choice!" and, "You have to take this!" I hated how I acted. Fellow cancer moms have told me they too have yelled about medications, but that doesn't absolve my disappointment in myself.

It took an hour and fifty minutes for Tucker to eventually finish the two teaspoons of liquid medicine. Damn, how I wished my son were able to swallow pills, but trying made him throw up. We were stuck in a vicious cycle of him nearly vomiting, causing more anxiety, causing more refusal, causing more chance of throwing up. Tucker was exhausted from the routine and the crying. I was exhausted and so angry that I didn't do better. I started crying and asked Tucker to please forgive me. My hug for him turned into us holding each other. We were both so incredibly sad.

But I couldn't let myself stay in this moment, because the girls were back home and needed reassurance too. I left Tucker to get Kayci and Siera ready for bed, and by the time I checked back, he was asleep.

Given that, I took the time to lie with my girls in their bunk beds. Kayci falls asleep more quickly, so my routine is to lie with her, rubbing her back until she is asleep, and then crawl down the ladder to lie with Siera in her bed while rubbing her tummy. It is amazing how much love can be stored in a mother's heart. All three of my children are my reasons for living. All three of them deserve protection from pain and suffering. But cancer was here now, so I needed to hold back the river of suffering like a dam and add joy to their small pond of life. Tomorrow, I would do just that. There was about to be a lot of joy, and no suffering allowed.

Chapter Eleven

For years, Tuesday evenings have been special for the A-Team. My mom started "Grandma-care" in 1994, when her first granddaughter was born. Mom took off one day a week to take care of her grandchildren. She spent eleven years doing this for the first five grandchildren, whom we call "the Big Five." After a few years off, I had Tucker, and Grandma-care reopened in February 2007, when I went back to work after maternity leave. Wow—at the time, I thought those were the hardest days of my life as a mom.

I did a good job of repopulating Grandma-care, with Kayci joining in 2008 and Siera in 2010. We were all delighted when more cousins were born to add to the fun. Mason was born in 2010, and Tucker was beyond thrilled to have another little boy in the family. Then came Olive in 2011, Paige in 2012, and Frances Mae (Frankie) in 2014. Grandma-care had become so busy that Papa had to take Tuesdays off to help. Tucker had been the main helper, since he was a big five-year-old and all the rest were babies.

Tucker hated when he started first grade and could no longer go to Grandma/Papa-care. My dad would meet me at the ISLA parking lot, and the girls would get into his car while Tucker and I went into school. Tucker was always sad those mornings. But we hurried out right after school to join the cousins and have that delicious homecooked meal that Mom made for everyone. I loved getting to see my siblings and in-laws as well as my parents. Every meal was finished with a round of ice cream. My parents never missed an opportunity to spoil their grandchildren—or their children, for that matter.

They would have a minimum of three, more likely six, different flavors of ice cream from which to choose. Tucker's task was to bring the other Littles down to the basement freezer and hand each one of them a container to bring up. He was the only one big enough to open the freezer and reach in to get things. Then the kids would take the orders from the adults, and Papa would scoop out the ice cream into the special ice cream dishes Mom had. Soon, the dozen or more of us were back around the table eating our ice cream, until the cousins scattered again to go play. We adults sat there visiting while listening to the laughter and joy, and sometimes tears from a crash or non-sharing incident. Some Tuesday nights, the Big cousins would stop by; on those nights, the Littles were in seventh heaven, since the Big Five (Amy, Sophie, Maggie, Hailey, and Henry) were their heroes.

Tucker's birthday celebration Tuesday was going to be the best Grandma/Papa-care night ever. Tucker got to spend the day with Grandma, Papa, and the two youngest Littles because his counts were still too low to attend school. He didn't mind missing school when there were cousins to play with, and Frankie and Paige were very happy to have him there with them for the day, as he was known to disregard the rule of TV time limits and no *SpongeBob*. Frankie and Paige sat by him while he showed them how to quietly break rules, but be polite and apologetic when/if caught.

Tucker had no idea that the entire A-Team was coming

to his birthday party. The big cousins came home from college for the party, and all eight aunts and uncles dropped what they were doing to come celebrate our special boy. We had Tucker's favorite dinner of grilled pork chops. Just like at every other grilling event, Tucker was Papa's grilling assistant. However, this time, my brothers had to help me get his wheelchair through the snow and around most of Grandma's flower gardens to the backyard. This is another example of "There's nothing we can't do." I had to bring extra blankets out there, and it wasn't easy getting him there, but cancer and wheelchairs weren't going to stop us from doing what we wanted to do and had always done. It's ironic that as a special education teacher and school psychologist, my career had been spent figuring out modifications that would allow students with differences to participate and succeed. Now that was my role as a mother. All the more reason for my conviction and determination to make this journey completely doable and successful.

After dinner, I surprised Tucker with the rally T-shirts I'd created. They were orange shirts with his phrase, "Team Tucker Go," and my slogan, "Together We Will Beat This." He LOVED them! "That's why you kept asking me what I wanted you to cheer!" Tucker said. *Yes, I and so many others will be cheering for you, in your words, and in your color.*

Kayci and Siera helped me hand out shirts to all twenty-two of us, plus Kevin and Dayra. Then Grandma brought out a very special "cake." Normally we have Dairy Queen ice cream cakes at family birthday parties, which Tucker never could enjoy with us because he didn't like chocolate. Well, Grandma created a special "ice cream" cake just for Tucker: it was made out of orange sherbet! Tucker squealed in his high voice: "Finally! Now I have an ice cream cake too!"

As he was inclined to do, Tucker quickly came up with a name for the confection: his DQG cake (Dairy Queen Grandma). His eyes were twinkling and his smile was bigger than usual. His heart, my heart, and the entire room were filled with happiness. There was no time or attention wasted on stupid cancer. Then we started singing "Happy Birthday," and Tucker was in the middle of an ocean of orange and a high tide of love.

That night, Tucker was the happiest I had seen him in weeks. As I lay in bed next to him, I almost started to let myself worry about whether this was his last birthday party, but I immediately rejected that idea. *Tucker and I are going to beat this thing,* I nearly said out loud. Then I picked up my phone to send a text to my siblings, in-laws, and parents. Finally, I let out the tears of joy that had been swelling up inside me all night as I thanked them for being there, supporting me and my children physically and emotionally.

My family of four is in a cocoon of love. It can't protect us from pain or bad things happening to us, but it can give us the warmth and shelter we need to grow through the suffering and come out a beautiful butterfly. And in Tucker's case, I knew he would turn into a bright, big, orange butterfly—a happy and healthy child.

Chapter Twelve

Wednesday was another good day, as Tucker got to come to school for a half day. I let him sleep in while I got the girls ready and over to school; Papa stayed home with him until I picked him up during my lunch break. Tucker loved going to school, and his classmates loved to see him. Actually, everyone did. The front office greeted him with huge smiles, and the administrators came out of their office to come welcome him before I even got him to his classroom.

As I rolled Tucker in, the place exploded with cheers while kids hustled to take over the wheelchair and help get him settled in. Then there was his teacher, Señora Shrestha, who always gave him a big hug; so much love exuded from her smile, eyes, and embrace. She always came to give me a hug too. That one was from a mom to a mom, nothing to do with her being my son's teacher or even being my coworker. She knew he was my sick little boy and that I was handing him over to her. That hug told me, "*I love him too and will take care of him as if he were my own.*" And with that, I could leave him.

Thursday morning, Papa had to drop off the girls while I brought Tucker to get his blood draw. We were getting down how to maneuver his wheelchair in and out of the small door and crooked sidewalk. The problem wasn't just the wheelchair—Tucker's right leg was in an immobilizer, stuck out straight in front of him. When I was pushing him, I was actually five feet behind where his toe was, and neither Tucker nor I could reach doors if we approached them straight on. The irony is not lost on me that for years I had told my kids that the handicap door buttons were not toys, that they should not think of them as fun but instead be grateful we didn't need them. Well, now we needed them.

Happy to have great counts, Tucker and I hurried to ISLA and found out he did not need any transfusions from this first round of chemo. This was excellent news, because the doctors told us that what happened in the first round was quite indicative of how Tucker would respond in subsequent rounds. Being the optimist I am, I was already planning on Tucker having minimal side effects and minimal days being stuck at home with low blood counts. I told him, "See, we've got this! You are kicking butt at this beating black Legos thing!"

The day got even better as Tucker's classmates celebrated his birthday with him. Curious George had to spend the day in my office, as Tucker was there to do his own work today. I loved being in my office knowing all three of my children were around me. It was awesome to say hi to each of them during their lunch periods. I had waited three years for this wonderful plan of having my children attend the school where I worked, and I was supposed to get four years like this. Just another reason we had no choice but to beat this.

The perfect day ended with a perfect night. Since the kids didn't have school on Friday, I brought them over to Sara's house for supper and a sleepover. It was amazing how our little kids adapted to Tucker in his wheelchair and brace. Without ever needing to be reminded, they brought him things he needed for whatever game they were playing, made extra room for him on the couch, and anticipated his needs and took care of them. All without pity or sadness. Their big brother/cousin had a different physical setup now, but he was exactly the same fun and hilarious kid. So inspiring.

As we headed into the weekend, great things continued. Friday night we got back to the rink—not on the ice, but we focused on what we could do, not what we couldn't. This was Jersey Night, where all the youth hockey players could attend the varsity game for free if they wore their hockey jerseys. Tucker went with his best sports buddies, Charlie and Greyson. Just like always, once I got him into the building, he was surrounded by friends excited to see him. What was new, however, was how they took over pushing his wheelchair and knew to have some kids walk in front to make sure people were out of the way and Tucker didn't bump his foot or leg on anything. These were eight- and nine-year-old little boys. Normally, that gender at that age shouldn't be in charge of anything vulnerable. But not these kids, not in this situation, and not with their favorite friend Tucker. Just like with the cousins, these boys could take care of him without pitying him or forgetting he needed to be careful, while still treating him like a regular kid. It was as impressive as it was heartwarming.

While Kayci, Siera, and I were busy selling wristbands in the lobby, I got word from the varsity team that they wanted Tucker to come to their locker room before the game. That was a total surprise. Neither Tucker nor I knew anyone on the high school teams. I went into the rink to find him—which wasn't hard to do, since he was always in the middle of the biggest cluster of kids—and brought him to the varsity locker room.

As Tucker entered the high school, players stood up and

applauded. They cheered for this little nine-year-old boy like he was a superstar. Then the captain presented him with a varsity jersey that had been signed by all of the players. They all shook Tucker's hand and said they were cheering for him and wanted him to come to more of their games. All this respect, support, and love from people who were strangers was amazing. They were teenagers, yet mature enough to recognize how to help in this unique situation.

Tucker put on the jersey; it went down past his knees, but he wore it proudly. His friends were there waiting for him outside the locker room. They were so excited to see the jersey and watch the game with their teammate and friend. It was a great night at the Hopkins Pavilion.

The awesome weekend continued on Saturday with Tucker's birthday party with his ISLA friends. Luckily, Tucker had always loved movies along with sports, so there were some activities that were not affected by being in a wheelchair. The fancy theaters with reclining seats were now perfect for Tucker's leg and immobilizer. Nearly all of his seventeen male classmates met us at the movie theater to celebrate. I was thrilled that so many boys attended despite getting invitations only sixty hours before the event. With cancer and blood counts, things can't be planned too far in advance. Definitely not how I liked to live life, but I adapted, and thankfully, so did everyone else. The boys' families dropped what they were doing and brought their sons to the theater, with gifts and all.

The positive energy was so awesome for Tucker. This was another experience where he was able to forget his limitations and be a kid hanging out with his friends. These boys loved Tucker, and I knew he could feel it.

Chapter Thirteen

Tucker felt great for five days, which made it so easy to forget about reality. However, cancer never goes too far away.

Saturday night, it was impossible to ignore the amount of hair that was floating around him while he took his bath. He called me into the bathroom and made his fingers like a strainer, lifting up clumps of hair to show me.

What does a mother say? I wanted to just cry. This made things so real for Tucker. I had seen scans and X-rays and way too many details that made this so horribly true for me. But Tucker hadn't. He had pain and a brace. Easy to ignore and just pretend, and wish, it was a sports injury. But when sitting in a bathtub of hair, that can only mean one thing: cancer. Stupid, evil, unrelenting cancer.

I knelt down on the bathroom floor and leaned over the tub to rub his back, immediately reminding me of the numerous baths I gave him during his infancy and toddler years. It was strange at first to be back in the bathroom with my nine-year-old. I was once again helping my child with the tasks of bathing, toileting, and getting dressed. Instead of only seeing the loss, I decided to see the connection that this ordeal was strengthening. Tucker once again needed his mom for these elementary tasks, which creates such a deep bond the first time a mother and child go through it. Thus the second time, while confronting the devil that is cancer, these routines grow and strengthen the bond from a sapling to a petrified tree.

As I knelt to rub Tucker's back and wipe his tears, I denied mine and said, "Well, isn't it great for you that you love to wear hats? And great for me that you are so adorable in hats! I will want to give you even more kisses!"

Tucker gave a huge "Ugh" right on cue. As I leaned over to kiss his head, he giggled and pretended to pull away. He loved snuggling with his mama but was never a huge fan of all the kisses. It was great to hear his laughter, and he even splashed some water at me. Now we were both laughing, which creates true joy in a mother's heart, especially a broken one.

As I helped him with his pajamas and tucked him into bed, Tucker told me it was hurting his head to have his hair fall out. I didn't know if this was physically true or not, as Tucker was so sensitive to pain. Either way, I told him he could choose what to do about it. "If you want to shave your head we can, or Lisa can cut it, or we can do it at the hospital the next time we go in. They apparently have a fun head-shaving area for kids. We should ask dad to shave his head too!" That made Tucker laugh. I reassured him that I already talked to the administration at ISLA, and he was going to be allowed to wear hats to school all day every day. How cool was it that he got to break the rules even more? He already got to be the only kid wearing sweatpants. Tucker knew I was just trying to cheer him up, and that none of this was "cool." But he decided to go with it and fell asleep as we talked about the movie and fun party. Distraction is key.

Tucker and I had one more week at home, and it was great to be together with the girls. Our foursome went to school each day and were home each night. I got to bring Siera to gymnastics and Kayci to her hockey. Siera loves all her time at the gym. At that time, she was on pre-team and had practice twice a week for two hours at a time. Kayci had hockey on weekends and once during the week. It was harder for her to enjoy hockey because her brother should have been there with her. They were one level apart, but their practices were back to back, so they always came and went together and watched each other play. Kayci didn't say it, but I knew she didn't feel right about getting to skate when her brother couldn't. Tucker supported her, as did the rest of the A-Team, so she tried her best to enjoy the sport she had loved since she was three.

At the end of the week, Tucker's hair was really falling out. This time, when he cried in my arms I didn't use distraction or humor. I just held him. I told him it wasn't fair and that he had every right to be sad and mad. I sat in bed holding him, rocking him gently, and watching his tears fall. Each one was a dagger in my heart.

It is so much more than the hair. My little boy was confronting the fact that he had cancer, knowing that cancer had killed a schoolmate last year. That cancer had killed the grandma he never got to meet. That his leg was in pain because of cancer. All the things I'd wanted to protect him from knowing for as long as I could. Now I couldn't keep those realities from him. No birthday parties could hide the reality that he was nearly bald because he had cancer and was putting poison into his body to try to stop it from killing him.

I know he was thinking all of that, and there was nothing I could do to protect him from this pain. Such a helpless feeling, which is the worst feeling a mother can have. Tucker cried himself to sleep. And then I did.

Luckily, Friday was a school day, which was a great distraction for Tucker. On Saturday, Kayci participated in the first ever all-girls pond hockey tournament. It was great to have many members of the A-Team come watch, with Kayci finally the center of attention. Getting Tucker's wheelchair out onto the massive ice rink was a challenge, as was keeping him from freezing, but "there's nothing we can't do." Tucker was loudly cheering for Kayci, which was awesome to watch. He had every right to be jealous and sad, to not want to watch, but that was not Tucker. He cared about her being happy, even more than himself.

Chapter Fourteen

Then Sunday night came, the ominous time when separation and pain loomed. I worked hard to distract and act normal, but all four of us knew that tomorrow we would be ripped apart from each other. Kayci and Siera would have Grandma, Papa, and Dayra to take care of them and would not see their mom or brother when they went to sleep at night. Tucker would have needles, isolation, and boredom surrounding him, reminding him he had cancer. I would be by my son's side, trying to decide which of my three children was hurting the most at any given moment. It was so depressing. All I could do was try to think of everything that would be sad or hard for each of my children and come up with a plan to counteract it.

For example, I knew the girls would be sad that I was not there in the morning, so I would ask Papa to bring them to McDonald's for a breakfast treat before school. They might be upset that they wouldn't see me in my office at ISLA, so I would write notes saying hi for Dayra to send in their lunch boxes. I knew Tucker would be miserable not being with friends and family, so I made a plan for different visitors to come every night or day he would be in the hospital. Long term, I worked with his teachers on a schedule for field trips and class parties to make sure they took place on days that Tucker would be in attendance, not in the hospital or home with low blood counts, so he wouldn't have to miss those wonderful events. I tried to circumvent every sadness that my three kids would encounter, not only to feel like I still had some control, but to distract from some of the sadness I had buried deep inside me.

Monday morning, I realized all the dread Sunday night had been warranted. Looking back at my CaringBridge post, I see that all I wrote for Tucker's first accessing of his port was, "Thank goodness that is over. That was hell because the poor boy freaked out." I don't know if I wanted to protect Tucker's privacy or just didn't want to relive it, but that entry is not AT ALL reflective of what "hell" it really was. And I don't need to try hard to remember it, as it is still so vivid over four years later. The real story is:

We went to the Journey Clinic to get Tucker's blood draw; then they told him he would get his port accessed there, in one of the recliners. Tucker put an end to that plan. No, he was not going to get accessed in the Journey Clinic. I wasn't sure why he didn't want it there, but I advocated for him and asked if we could change protocol. The social worker was hesitant at first, but I convinced her that since he was going to need to end up in his hospital room anyway, why couldn't we just do that first? She agreed.

We got in our room/apartment and unpacked. The male nurse, Jimbo, ended up being one of Tucker's favorites, as he was funny, had lots of stories to tell, and loved hockey. Today, however, when he rolled the tray of accessing paraphernalia into the room and parked it next to Tucker's bed, Tucker saw the needles and screamed.

I had been standing beside him, holding his hand, but that wouldn't suffice. I tried to calm him, as did Judd, Kevin, and Jimbo. I put the TV on and focused Tucker on the program;

that wasn't overly helpful, as daytime TV is so dumb, but I tried. Jimbo started the first step of wiping the area of the chest with disinfectant. Tucker was screaming again. The smell was repugnant and very upsetting to him. With his yelling and anxiety, I feared he would throw up. I grabbed Tucker's blankie and held it over his nose, but he was pulling away and moving his arms. Jimbo told us that if anything touched the area, he would have to start over and disinfect again.

I was not going to let this process start over, so I climbed into the bed behind Tucker and, as lovingly as I could, hugged him tightly enough to restrain his arms. There was no doubt Tucker felt this, which made me so sad. Now we had the CFL therapist there helping too, trying in vain to distract Tucker with iPad games and telling him it would be OK. At that point, I knew my son was not going to calm down.

I started setting guidelines and told him that when he yelled at everyone to stop, we would, but only for thirty seconds; then we had to start again. Jimbo got the needles ready, and Tucker lost it. We stopped once, and I used that time to get my arms wrapped around his arms and my calves on top of his legs. This had to get done, and my son was beyond rational. I told the nurse to proceed, but Tucker was able to kick my legs off his. I directed Judd to hold down one leg and the nurse's assistant to hold down the other leg. This poor boy was a hog-tied animal, yelling and crying as three adults held him still. It was beyond awful. But I was going to get this done.

I shouted directions over Tucker's yelling, and Jimbo inserted the first needle. Tucker let out a scream like he had just been stabbed in the gut. I ignored it and told Jimbo to get the second needle, now. I told everyone to stop talking to Tucker, as he was in a panic attack, and the more words and voices the worse it was going to be. "Everyone just hold onto his body, and Jimbo, get that damn needle in!" I directed.

The second needle was harder than the first, causing Jimbo to give it a forceful shove. This was inches from my face, and I wanted to cry when I saw how hard he had to push it into Tucker's chest. I told the men they could let go of Tucker's legs, but I knew I had to keep *restraining* his arms. The nurse had to get the huge adhesive covering over the port and get the lines just right. Tucker's moving would slow down this process and possibly hurt him if he nudged the needles. Plus, I had to keep his mask on him and mine on me, because right now his body was exposed where the needles entered. Tucker, who thought it felt like he was suffocating under the mask, continued to yell.

Finally, the adhesive was on and I could let go of him—actually, I could stop restraining him. I didn't let go of him. I stayed there for nearly an hour as he laid back on my chest, rubbing his arms and caressing his cheeks. He was exhausted, and when my adrenaline surge went down, I was too.

Judd found an Alaskan wildlife show on the TV. Judd loves hunting and being out in the woods, and Tucker liked these shows too. Eventually, he was calm, and I got out from behind him. I went into the bathroom to shut my eyes and collect myself.

Oh my god. Did that really just happen? And how am I going to get Tucker through this so many more times over the next nine months?

I didn't have the time to answer either of those questions; I just stayed numb and rejoined my son in the room. He wanted to go sit in the recliner. I could relate—that bed had just been the site of a war.

After moving him to the recliner, I apparently took time to make that CaringBridge post. Obviously, I was not ready to acknowledge what had just transpired over the past hour, so I summed it up as "hell" because my "poor boy was freaked out." Sure, that was it.

The rest of Monday went *much* better. Tucker moved from the recliner to the couch and explained that he didn't like being in the bed because it made him think he was sick. The couch was right next to the big window so it was cooler for Tucker, who always ran warm—plus, we could see all the holiday lights on the downtown buildings. It was December 14, so Christmas was right around the corner. I was not sure how I was going to get all Santa's shopping done, since Tucker and I would be in the hospital that week and the following week. I would only have three days out of the hospital before Christmas.

Also stressful—actually *more* stressful—was that there was a chance we would not get out by Christmas. The twenty-fifth was a Friday, and best-case scenario was leaving on Thursday, Christmas Eve. *I can't have Tucker in the hospital on Christmas Eve*, I thought. However, I knew I would figure something out if it did happen.

Tucker's physical therapist, Erin, came in that afternoon and told him she was thrilled with his progress. Lisa had been coming over to do PT with Tucker a few times a week, and it was helping him a lot. I had made some progress too. I decided I would leave Tucker for a couple hours on Tuesday evenings when Kayci and Siera were over at Grandma/Papa-care night.

Tucker told me he wanted me to go so I could bring back some of Grandma's awesome suppers.

I think he knew I needed his blessing if I were to ever leave his hospital room. He was so wise and could read me and others so well. It would be great to see Kayci and Siera on Tuesdays, as I already missed them by Monday evenings. Next, I made a plan that after Siera's gymnastics on Wednesday, Kevin would bring the girls to the hospital to visit me and Tucker. Then we planned to be home Thursdays. See, we could get through this.

Chapter Fifteen

Wednesday, December 16, was a day we will never forget, the happiest day Tucker ever had in the hospital. That was the day Wild players came to Masonic to meet kids in the lobby and visit a few patients in their rooms.

I still don't know who, but someone contacted the Wild to tell them about Tucker and his utter devotion to the team. Because this kind person took the time to make this request, I received a call letting me know that Tucker would be lucky enough to receive a personal visit in his room. I was grateful and thrilled.

The Wild rep asked who Tucker's favorite player was—that was an easy question. Tucker's favorite player was Jason Zucker. He wasn't a captain or even a top player on the team at that time, but Tucker loved his speed and how he passed to his linemates. Tucker also admitted to me that he initially liked Zucker because their names rhymed, though it turns out they don't when "Zucker" is pronounced correctly. I was very hopeful Zucker would be stopping by, but I knew Tucker liked all the other players, so anyone else would be great too. (Well, he did also like Jared Spurgeon a little more than everyone else—his birthday was the day before Tucker's.)

On that magical day, when the CFL worker confirmed that the Wild would be coming to the room, I told Tucker, who had to hold in his screams of delight. My sister Sara was bringing

Mason to visit, because it would be even more fun for Tucker if he could share this with the person who was the closest thing he had to a brother. Despite being only five, Mason loved the Wild as much as Tucker did. Sara, Mason, Judd, Kevin, and Tucker sat anxiously as they waited for one of the team to arrive.

Then it happened: Jason Zucker walked through the door!

Tucker was thrilled but able to keep his cool. Mason could hardly speak. The first thing Tucker did was give Jason the shirt that we had made for him. It was one of his Tucker rally shirts that a friend in St. Michael had designed and distributed to his fans in their community. On the back, we had written the name "Tucker," then crossed the "T" out and put a "Z" above it. I remember Jason being a little shocked, and later found out it was the first time a patient had given him a gift.

Well, he wasn't done being surprised. Zucker sat down with Tucker and found himself in a very detailed conversation about how the Wild were doing, how Jason was doing, and what head coach Mike Yeo should have the team work on. Jason had started with the typical question of "Who is your favorite player?"—when Tucker reported the birthdates, years on the team, and points many players had, Jason learned that the kid he was talking to was no ordinary fan. We would later find out that Jason was no ordinary player.

Jared Spurgeon was with Zucker for the visit. When they are beside each other in their Wild jerseys, both Zucker and Spurgeon seem like your regular NHL players, except with perfect teeth. Only when Kevin, who is six feet tall, shook their hands did I realize they were a little smaller than one would expect—he was notably taller than either of them. Tucker made it clear that any lack of height meant they were just that much more talented. I fully agree.

Spurgeon sat down with Mason and was surprised to fall into a discussion about the Wild's current standings in the league and how many points the other teams were ahead of them. When he and Zucker gave the boys blankets that had all the NHL team logos on them, they stood there with their mouths open as Mason and Tucker proceeded to name the team name of each logo. Tucker could have spent the whole day talking Wild hockey and breaking down the games with the guys. I was bursting with so much joy from seeing my son be so happy. I had always heard of professional athletes making hospital visits, but I had no idea how much joy they bring. Not only was Tucker the happiest he had been in the last two months, this was the most exciting day of his life.

Unfortunately, the visit with Spurgeon and Zucker had to end, but the fun wasn't over. Getting Tucker in his wheelchair, our group went down to the lobby to see the other players that were visiting. I only knew Ryan Suter and Mikael Grandlund (oh my goodness, Suter is even cuter in person!); Tucker had to tell me the other players' names, which he did easily. When he visited with the team, they were all surprised to discuss their game and season in such detail with a nine-year-old fan. Mason was still in awe of everyone and had less to say because of it.

It was so awesome to see Tucker in the middle of such a great group of men, and it was so wonderful to see them enjoy talking with the young boys. Suter told me he had a son Tucker's age and couldn't imagine what I was going through. I told him that this was helping both me and Tucker tremendously and thanked him for doing these visits. He was very genuine, as were all the other Wild players, who stated that they truly enjoyed coming to meet kids and had huge admiration for them and the battles they wage against deadly diseases. Such great men. Almost as great as my little man.

That night, as I lay next to Tucker in his bed, rubbing his bald head, he said, "Mom, there is one good thing about cancer. You get to meet your sports hero." I hugged him and shed happy tears, a very welcome change.

To make this story even more incredible, I found out a year later that Jason never got the message that he was supposed to go to Tucker's room. Four players were in the elevator and asked which floor they wanted to go to. Zucker spoke for him and Spurgeon and said, "Floor Five." Fate stepped in—these two were destined to meet.

Tucker was discharged the following night and was very excited to go to school on Friday wearing his signed Wild jersey. He told his friends all about hanging out with Zucker and Spurgeon and meeting the other players. Tucker's classmates were so happy for their friend. It was another great day.

Chapter Sixteen

On December 20, Sunday-night dread took over my heart. At a time when children should be thinking about presents and a break from school, my children were thinking about separation, needles, and cancer. This time I didn't have the distraction of packing up because I'd left everything how we'd brought it home just three nights ago. All the pictures colored by Mason, Paige, Olive, and Frankie; the cards from classmates; the Team Tucker Go posters created by the sixth graders; and the mini Christmas trees were in containers and set to go.

I did have the distraction of trying to wrap Santa presents. All three of my kids still believed in Santa Claus, and I was not going to let cancer ruin that too. The problem was I didn't know where Santa would get to deliver the presents. Of course, I would do everything in my power to get the T out of Tucker's little body in time to come home. But I knew I had met my match when it came to having my plans work out, no matter how hard I worked, so I made sure I had an air mattress ready to go in case the girls needed to come sleep at the hospital with us Christmas Eve. I didn't know where we would wake up Christmas morning, but I did know the four of us would be together.

Monday morning, I was dreading getting Tucker to the hospital. This time he knew what accessing was, and he was already full of anxiety. He was also horribly sad that he was missing another week of school. He hated being away from his friends, and this time it would be two weeks in a row. Tucker didn't need to be reminded that with winter break, it was actually going to be four weeks before he got to go back to ISLA, his best escape from cancer. I called Dr. Weigel's assistant and told her we wouldn't be there at 9:00 a.m. I could tell Tucker was about to break down crying, and I wasn't going to let that visual stick in his sisters' minds throughout the week. It probably isn't normal to tell a doctor what time works for you, but I am not normal. These were my children, and I needed to put them first.

However, I also couldn't delay long, because the sooner the T got started, the better chance we would have to get home on Christmas Eve. There were so many factors to consider and three little children to protect. I focused on the girls and got them ready for school with my undivided attention, leaving Tucker to hang out on the couch watching *Teen Titans Go!* or *Scooby-Doo.* After I gave the girls the longest hugs I could and sent them with Papa, I knew I had to figure out how to get Tucker to the hospital without having a panic attack. I failed.

Tucker started crying and yelling that he wasn't going to go. I tried relaxation techniques, pressing on his "third eye" (the center spot between one's eyebrows) and telling him all the visitors I had arranged for him that week. I also reminded him the sooner we got in there, the sooner we could leave. After five minutes, he was still just as upset, so I had to take action. Kevin had already loaded the stuff in his car, so I told him to grab Tucker's coat and hold the doors open. Both Tucker and Kevin were surprised when I placed a blanket on my son, then lifted him up and started carrying him out of the house.

Tucker was yelling at me to put him down, screaming, "No, Mommy!" As I got to the door, he grabbed the doorframe and wrapped the tips of his little fingers around it. I tried to take another step, but he got his other hand on it too. I can still see his nails turn white from the pressure. I told Kevin to help me; I couldn't keep holding on. He took some of the weight, and one by one I peeled Tucker's fingers off the doorframe while he screamed into my face, crying, "No, Mommy! Don't make me go there!"

I hurried to open the back door of the car, and Kevin placed him on the seat. Since Tucker needed to keep his leg extended across the seat, I ran to get in the front seat and yelled to Kevin to hurry up and start driving. He wasn't quick enough. Tucker had opened the back door and was trying to get out. I jumped out of the car and got in the back seat, pulling Tucker in and reaching over to shut the door, bumping Tucker's leg and causing him to scream even louder. Tears were streaming down his face. Kevin said he would get out to close the door, and I yelled, "No! You have got to start driving!"

As I got the door shut, the car was moving. At the stop sign, Tucker lunged for the door handle again. "Keep driving and lock the doors!" I yelled. Once again, I was restraining my child. I had to manhandle my bald, weak, cancer-ridden son to keep him safe. It was worse than a horror movie.

Five minutes later, which felt like thirty, we were on the highway and Tucker no longer reached for the door locks or handles. I held his phone for him to play games or watch a video. I also continued to hold him, not only to hug him but to be ready in case he made a move for the door again.

Tucker remained calm until we reached the exit ramp and he saw the bright colors of the U of M Masonic Hospital. The screams started again, and he made another attempt to open the door. I held him and prayed the light would be green so we didn't have to stop. It wasn't.

But then something amazing happened. When Tucker saw a homeless man with a cardboard sign asking for help, he instantly stopped yelling. He turned to me and asked for money. I said, "I don't even know where my purse is, honey." This was true, but I mostly just didn't want to let go of him in case he tried to get out of the car.

Tucker insisted this time, "Mom, we need to give him some money."

Kevin found my purse in the front seat and gave a five-dollar bill to Tucker, who rolled down his window, handed it to the man, and told him to have a good day. The man's eyes filled with gratitude as he replied, "God bless you," and told Tucker to have a nice day too. If he knew where this sweet little boy was headed, the man would have been even more grateful.

As soon as we rolled up the window, the anxiety came back like Tucker had flipped a switch. He cried and yelled the rest of the way to the hospital. Kevin pulled up to the front doors, and I held my son as he got out the wheelchair. Judd was there waiting inside the lobby and came out. Tucker wanted to always show strength in public and in front of his father, so he stopped screaming as we opened the car door.

Part of me was jealous that Judd and others never had to endure the pain of Tucker's screams nor pry his sweet little fingers from doorframes. But I accepted that if I wanted to be in the trenches with Tucker every step of the way, witnessing every moment of his pain came with that duty. This duty became an honor. I was grateful to have the opportunity to be in these lows with Tucker, because it gave me the opportunity to fix them. I am also grateful because there is a bond that was created that no one else will ever have with him—a bond that transcends time and distance.

The accessing routine was the same as before. Tucker tried to remain calm, but anxiety doesn't wait for an invitation. As soon as the needles came in, so did the panic. This time I was prepared, and even though we had a different nurse, I was able to prepare her and direct her through the screams and tears. I was sitting behind Tucker in the bed, restraining his arms. I had his blankie ready to cover his nose and was able to tell the nurse that if she knew what was good for her and everyone in this room, she would not uncover those needles until I had Tucker looking absolutely in the other direction.

It was hell, again. The second needle was hard to push in, again. Both Tucker and I were exhausted, again. I lay there in bed, his little body on top of me, and did my recovery there. It was 1:00 p.m. I had been dealing with anxiety, tears, and fears from my three children since 8:00 a.m. I was emotionally spent and wondered how I would recharge in time for another four days of intermittent sleep, worry about getting out for Christmas Eve, and manage my children's emotions as well as my own.

Lisa, that's how. She was who I called when I brought my toddlers into a steamy bathroom to treat their croup, the one who counseled me whether or not to bring them to a doctor or ER, and the one who checked in with me every day I or my children were recovering from some ailment, just as she did for every member of the A-Team. The oldest story I know that shows Lisa's maternal essence comes from when she was two-and-a-half years old; Mom tells me that walking through the airport, she insisted that she hold her little brother's hand so he didn't get lost. She has never stopped offering to hold our hands.

Lisa left work to visit Tucker every single day he was in the hospital. If she couldn't come during the day, she came early in the morning and left us a donut that we would wake up to find. She attended every meeting and followed up with doctors in her hospital to make sure everything checked out. She also collaborated with Tucker's physical therapist and came to my house to give him extra therapy between hospitalizations, which saved him from having more time out of school.

Of course, she also volunteered to give Tucker his shots. I had to restrain him while she injected him. Sometimes Tucker started to cry when he saw her walk into our home, fearing she was there for a shot. Once when she returned from the kitchen with the needle, Tucker was no longer on the couch. After searching, Lisa found him in the back corner of a closet, hiding from her. This hurt her heart, but never slowed her down from taking excellent care of her nephew.

That night, Lisa surprised Tucker when she walked in with her daughters, Sophie and Maggie, along with Kayci and Siera. Lisa and her girls are the queens of crafting—they brought projects, and together they and the kids made Christmas presents for the grandparents. I sat on the couch, shutting my eyes and listening to the laughter. I would have liked to have been involved, but this was my chance to recharge and rest. Lisa was the only other person besides me and Judd that Tucker would let help him with the urinal bottle, so I even got a break from two rounds of that. It was the couple hours of rest I needed to move past the hell of that morning and be ready for three more sleepless nights.

Chapter Seventeen

Tuesday morning, Tucker and I started the day with the new routine we'd created together. I would set my alarm for 9:55 a.m. so I could grab a Diet Dew, get the TV on, and wake up Tucker for our favorite daytime show, *The Price Is Right.* Tucker and I always slept in, as we are both night owls. Once he fell asleep around 11:30 each night, I would work on my special ed paperwork for a couple hours. In the mornings, we hoped the doctors wouldn't come until after *The Price Is Right* ended. If they did stop in, I would ask if there was anyone else they had yet to see and if they could come back any time after eleven o'clock. Some thought I shouldn't do that, but my son only had a few hours where he was absolutely content in that place he hated, so I was going to work to protect those times.

Soon all the doctors and nurses did their best to avoid stopping in during *The Price Is Right.* If they did, they waited for a commercial to start talking to us. They also knew not to come in during a Wild game. They were awesome. Many staff members of the hospital came to recognize us, because Tucker usually gave them a smile and I was always wearing orange. Every Monday Tucker and I had our Team Tucker Go shirts on, and every subsequent day I had another orange shirt or sweatshirt on. When my family came to visit Tucker, they always had their Team Tucker Go shirts on as well. I later learned that the security guards at the front desk stopped asking, "What floor?" when they saw my family in their orange shirts and just automatically said, "Floor Five?"

After *The Price Is Right* that day, Tucker was pretty crabby and tried to refuse going on our daily trip to the cafeteria. I didn't eat their food very often—I usually ate Tucker's free meal, since he either wasn't hungry or was craving other food. But I did love the cafeteria's fountain Diet Coke, my treat every day and a nice break from the room.

I got Tucker to go on our outing, but after we got back, he wanted to sit in the bed. That was another sign that something was wrong, so I crawled in next to him and asked him if he was having a bad morning. My mother's intuition was right. Tucker instantly broke down into tears and laid his head on my chest. He cried, "It's not fair! It's not fair!"

I held him and agreed. "Yes, it isn't fair. And you have every right to be sad."

"I want to do things! I miss sports! This was supposed to be my year to play Minors A [in baseball]. And I miss playing hockey!"

My heart broke, again. Even though I was happy that we were most likely going to get through this with my son's life and limbs, *"At least you get to live"* isn't an effective pep talk for a nine-year-old. I told him we didn't know about baseball; he might be able to participate in it, at least to some extent. And maybe he would be able to skate a little this summer. It was good that I fully believed that—Tucker could sense that I did and thus believed it a little himself.

I did not, however, tell him that he wouldn't be able to swim in the lake at his grandpa's cabin that summer. He wouldn't be able to go tubing with his sisters and cousins. Nor could I tell him that he would still be in the hospital two to three weeks a month in the summer. If he was bored and sad now because of how much other kids got to do in the two weeks of winter break, how would the ten weeks of summer break feel for him? Oh my gosh, I was so grateful that I hadn't let Dr. Weigel or anyone else tell him all this other bad news. As a school psychologist who had handled lots of students' bad news and situations, I knew a child can only take so much at one time. I, an adult, could hardly absorb and deal with the amount of loss that Tucker would experience over the coming year.

In this moment, I told him that while it was true that he didn't get to do what other kids were doing, he did get to do a few things that they didn't get to. Other kids don't get to meet their favorite player, like he got to meet Jason Zucker. This visit was a gift that kept on giving to my sweet, sad boy. When his tears slowed down, I reminded him that I knew someone who could get emails to the players. I asked him if he wanted to email Zucker and the others. Tucker looked up. It had been an hour of him crying onto my chest, and it was finally coming to an end.

I got out of bed to get my computer, and we started an email. Soon he was on his NHL app on his phone, reminding me which players had scored in each game that week. He described Zucker's recent goal in his email to Jason. Then he wanted to email Jason Pominville to tell him that they shared a birthday on November 30 and thank him for scoring a goal on that day for his present.

This lifted Tucker's spirits. Then he asked if he would get to go to a Wild game. I told him I would look into it and try to find some tickets.

People had warned me that it would be hard to ask for help. Not for me, it wasn't. Not when that was how I could make my children happier. I got on Facebook and CaringBridge and asked anyone to help me get some Wild tickets. That would be a perfect antidote for the next round of tears, as Tucker rightfully cried that this wasn't fair.

Judd arrived after all this had transpired. It wouldn't have worked for me to explain it to him, so I just told him it would be good to keep things light and play some Xbox with Tucker. It was Tuesday, and I was going to go to Grandma/Papa-care night and pick up the girls. School was out for winter break, so we were going to have a sleepover at the hospital. It was a lot of work bringing the girls and their stuff, but eventually we got the air mattress to fit and all blown up. Judd decided to stay that night too, so I slept in the recliner next to my boy, looking down at my girls on the air mattress. It was tricky to do all the urinal trips with so much less space, but I was a pro at that now.

It was good for that day to come to an end—I was exhausted. I liked to keep busy caring for Tucker, helping Kayci and Siera feel equally as important, running my household, and maintaining all my job's tasks and paperwork. I was lucky to be so crazy; the alternative was sitting there feeling the sadness Tucker felt along with my own, like we'd endured today. That was horrible, painful, and something I couldn't keep living through. I needed to stay positive and upbeat. Not just to show my children everything would work out, but to show myself too.

Thankfully, Wednesday and Thursday were better days for Tucker, and thus for me. I stepped up my job as his social secretary and reached out to more people to come visit him. Tucker felt trapped, and the only way to distract him was by having friends and family come play with him. I made him walk, move, and drink extra fluids, even when he tried to tell me no. It was difficult to wrap my mind around being strict, bossy, and even scolding to my sick child. My natural instinct was to just hold him and let him do whatever was most comfortable. But I couldn't do that, frustratingly. I had to push him to exercise when he didn't want to, to take medicines he hated; hell, I had to restrain him so he could have needles shoved into his chest.

This is not anyone's idea of motherhood, and certainly nothing a woman thinks about when she envisions taking care of the life that is growing inside her once they finally arrive. However, it does correspond with the natural instinct to keep your child alive, the instinct of knowing what is best for them. I knew Tucker would be devastated to spend Christmas morning in the hospital and would feel even worse that he made that happen for his little sisters. So, I took on the role of drill sergeant to make things happen that would benefit my children, even though it felt horrible.

Being "mean" worked again. Tucker got the T processed through him by 5:00 p.m. on Thursday, Christmas Eve. I packed up as quickly as I could and called Kevin to come get us. Tucker called Kayci and Siera to tell them the great news: we would all be home for Christmas Eve and Christmas morning.

I was thrilled to tuck in all three of my children after we set out the cookies for Santa. Tucker always made sure we set out some food that the reindeer would like too. (I still had hope he wouldn't be a hunter.) I had all the kids sleep in my bed so the girls could sleep with their brother. The girls also missed sleeping next to me, especially little Siera. Until October, the kids had taken turns sleeping in my bed with me. Since then, as Siera would say with a very sad voice, "Tucker gets all the turns." But that night was everyone's turn.

I put Tucker's right leg on the edge so no one bumped it, Kayci next to him, and Siera on her sister's other side. I was going to sleep across the bottom of the bed, but with the duty and honor of being Santa, I wasn't going to get much sleep anyway—there was a lot of wrapping left to do. I hadn't gotten much sleep the previous nights, but this was a much better setting and reason for sleep deprivation.

Chapter Eighteen

It's hard for me to write about Christmas morning. Hell, it's hard for me to write this entire book. I remember being determined to make this a great day, just like every other Christmas my kids had experienced. This year one of them was bald and required my help to walk to the tree, that was all.

The kids were excited and woke up early. First, they got down their stockings and took turns emptying them. Then, they took turns opening the presents under the tree. Somehow Santa always got them exactly the same number of presents, so no one "gets more than me!" Tucker was the perfect big brother, always patient for his turn and cheering the gifts of his sisters. I swear he got more joy from other people being happy than he did from his own happiness, just like his mommy. Tucker was funny and hammed up his reactions to his gifts. He got lots of hats, which he put on right away. He was finally getting used to his bald head in the house, but still never took his hat off in public.

While the kids played with their gifts, I made our favorite Pillsbury cinnamon rolls. I didn't want to have to limit any of us, so I made two tubes. Tucker then made his specialty: scrambled eggs. He'd started cracking eggs by age three and took over making our scrambled eggs by age seven. At our family week at the cabin each summer, he made them for the entire A-Team. As usual, he did a great job and they were delicious.

Every Christmas, we go to my parents' house for the evening. That way, every family has time for Santa in the morning. Tonight was no exception—we arrived around 4:00 p.m. for appetizers, filled the house with chatter, and finished prep for the delicious feast that Mom and Dad prepared for us. Dad grilled steaks, and Mom prepared crab legs. The sisters and Ryan's wife, Katie, helped with all the sides. My favorite side is our Anderson potatoes. Oh my gosh, so good!

When it was time for grilling to start, of course Papa needed his number-one assistant, so I got Tucker to the front door and, with help, wheeled him through the snow to the backyard. I tried to make it funny with noises, but something was bubbling up inside me. Luckily, my older brother Mark was with me and did most of the pushing when I couldn't get Tucker through. Mark stayed as third-in-command and grilled with his dad and his nephew.

Instead of going in the back door, I walked around to the front. After passing by the windows, I retreated behind a bush by the garage. There was something wrong. I had to stop. Not just stop walking back into the house—I had to stop smiling. I had to stop pretending. I had to . . . cry.

This wasn't like all the other Christmases. This one sucked. This one, my son was in a wheelchair and had a port in his chest and cancer in his leg and lungs. This Christmas was scary. So scary.

What if this is . . . Tucker's last one? The sobbing was so loud and the heartache was causing physical pain in my chest. *My son has cancer. A bad one. And there is a chance he won't survive. There is a chance that this is his last Christmas. No!*

I tried so hard, but I couldn't stop crying. I couldn't stand. My lungs were exhausted from crying so hard, and my legs were too weak to hold me. I crouched down, leaning against the garage with my forehead against my knees. Crying. Worrying. Thinking the worst. Exactly what I didn't want to do, especially today. My mind went to a vision of Christmas with only Siera and Kayci in front of the tree. *God, make this stop! Why can't I get my thoughts and visions back under control? Please!*

I don't know how long I'd been out there—probably twenty minutes or so—when Mark's wife, Jenny, walked up to me. She asked me if I wanted a coat—very astute of her to not ask what was wrong. Then she just hugged me. I didn't want anyone to see me like that. My plan was to always hide my fears and be strong so that people could just focus on and worry about Tucker, Kayci, and Siera; not me. Thus, it was perfect that out of everyone, Jenny was the one who found me. Not my parents, who would have been broken to see their daughter like this; same with my sisters and brothers. And I was so glad it wasn't any of the kids, especially Tucker. Jenny knew pain and loss, as her parents and a sibling had died of cancer. She could convey an understanding of my fears, but also was kind to remind me of my strength and how well I was doing taking care of all three of my children.

I don't remember her words, but I do remember regaining my strength. Jenny went back inside and said the phrase I had heard from so many wonderful people: "I don't know how you do it." To be honest, I still don't know either. But for that many people to say that to me, I must have been "doing it." And it wasn't time to stop. It was Christmas, a time for family and love.

My entire family is inside right now, and they will all be here next year too. I went in to join them. The food was delicious, especially the steak. *My son is an excellent griller.* I was sure he would even be better next year, when he walked to the grill on his own.

With my resolve reestablished, I worked hard to be present. For minutes in a row I ate, talked, and laughed with family without thinking about cancer. The twenty-two of us plus Kevin were around the table, enjoying the feast. I had a second glass of wine, hoping to extend the few minutes of escaping reality and make the laughs a little heartier. It didn't work; part of me was still so very sad. My mind could not stop returning to the thought that had been haunting me all day: *What if this is the last Christmas with my son?*

I fought the urge to keep Tucker by my side at all times, trying to indulge myself with so much of him I would feel full, like I had enjoyed my son "enough." Everyone wanted their fill of this amazing boy, so I had to share. Besides, I was afraid that Tucker would sense my fears and thoughts if I kept him too close to me. So, he sat on the couch or floor surrounded by his cousins, laughing with his Littles and being waited on by the Big Five. I sat watching him, telling myself to be content with the view and sounds of all the interactions.

It was so hard to share him. That sounds horrible, and I am ashamed that was how I felt. I'm glad I hid that from everyone—at least I hope I did. But Tucker either sensed something or was feeling the same for me, because when it was time to find seats for gift opening, he asked, "Can someone help me sit by my mom?"

I wanted to burst into tears again. Out of a room of his favorite people, I was his most favorite, and he wanted to indulge in some Mom-time. Even if this book were a thousand pages, I could not explain how much I love my boy.

Tucker leaned against me the entire gift opening. I had never been so thrilled with our family rule of one person opening a gift at a time—I didn't want that night to end. Just in case.

Chapter Nineteen

On the afternoon of December 26, the kids went to Judd's to celebrate with him and their Helstrom family. I don't know how I got through it, though I would guess it involved going out with Kevin, a number of cocktails, and lots of sleep. I tried to tell myself that it was a good thing to have these breaks when they were at their dad's so I could recharge, but my heart yearned for them every minute they were away.

However, I did need the sleep and emotional rest, as Monday morning would be another horrible drive to the hospital for our third week of chemo in a row. Not only that, the chemo covered both weeks of winter break, a time that is filled with playing, friends, and family for most kids. But not for Tucker. Like I predicted, Monday didn't go well.

The next night didn't either. I didn't write a journal entry for the following night, December 30, but I won't ever forget it. That night, Sara and Ryan brought the Little cousins to visit, which helped, but Tucker was still very down. It didn't help that there wasn't a Wild game to distract him; all he could think about was everyone else playing, skating on the neighborhood pond, and sledding in the new-fallen snow. As the cousins left, Tucker started crying and yelling, "It isn't fair!" He even tried to get out of bed, despite the pain of moving his leg without help. That made the cries louder, and my poor nieces and nephew could hear Tucker's sobs as they walked out of the room.

I tried all my tricks—turning on the TV, finding a movie, reassuring him it was just one more day until he could get out, and moving him to the couch. But nothing worked. And that last choice made things worse. Tucker pressed his face against the window and realized if he looked down, he could see the cars leaving the underground parking ramp. He sobbed, "I want to go too!" as each car left. Then, he saw Sara's car leaving and started screaming. I don't know how a mother's heart can handle this, but it can't for long.

I called the nurse and insisted that Tucker get some anti-anxiety meds in his IV right now. I knew he was in a panic attack, experiencing emotional pain beyond my ability to fix, and I certainly didn't want to wait it out. I don't remember how the nurse responded; it was hard to hear over Tucker's sobs. I do remember insisting that he get it, and now.

She returned with the meds and added them to his IV drip. Eventually Tucker stopped yelling and was crying quietly. I was sitting beside him on the couch, and he was leaning against my chest, his tears dripping onto my shirt. I put on a movie as I rubbed his back. Finally, he started watching it. The tears stopped. I was grateful the horrible forty-five minutes were over.

Just then Tucker's phone rang, and he saw that it was a call from his dad. Instantly the tears were back. "It's not fair!"

I could not believe the timing. I grabbed my phone to text Judd to stop calling, but my pleas were ignored. As I tried to text the reasons why, Tucker just held his phone and sobbed, "I know they're all skating and I can't! Everyone is having fun but me!"

I told Judd what was happening, but he wanted to talk to Tucker, thinking he could make it better. He wanted to put the girls on the phone to talk to him too. I could not make him understand that all of them represented what Tucker was being denied. Cancer chose him—he did nothing wrong, but he was stuck in a hospital, bald, in pain, and locked away from his life as a nine-year-old child. Everyone else that he knew had that life, and he couldn't take it anymore.

Judd refused to believe that things were that bad and kept calling. I ended up turning off both of our phones and putting them in the closet. I was so angry, but I had to keep control and stay calm. Anxiety feeds anxiety, and I had to get Tucker calmed down, again.

Oh, it was a painful evening. Thursday's discharge could not come soon enough. And the two-week break from chemo and hospitalizations was very badly needed.

Chapter Twenty

Finally, there was something fun for Tucker to experience and enjoy. The St. Michael-Albertville girls' basketball team honored Tucker at their game on Tuesday, January 5.

Medically, the timing couldn't have been worse. Mondays through Wednesdays, Tucker's blood counts bottomed out, leaving him the most susceptible to germs. His doctors were quite concerned about him going to a high school gymnasium full of people. I was concerned too, but I was also worried about Tucker's mental health. He had missed out on so much over break and the past two months. Not only did he have anxiety, but I was seeing signs of depression as well. I negotiated with the doctors and made a plan. I asked if we could do an extra blood draw on Tuesday to see how things looked compared to Monday. I also had Judd talk with the coach and rope off an area on the side of the gym opposite the bleachers for Tucker and his family to sit. I fully acknowledged this might cause Tucker to get a fever and need to go to the ER, but it was a small risk I was willing to take for the gain of his emotional well-being. Finally, I got the doctor's approval and packed up Kayci, Siera, and Tucker to bring them up to St. Michael for the game.

All the negotiating and extra work was worth it. Tucker's Helstrom family—Kris, Jeff, cousins Anna and Maren, and Grandpa Gary—were there, along with hundreds of people from the St. Michael-Albertville community. Everyone dressed in orange. Even the players from the home team *and* the away team had orange shirts on for their pregame warm-up. It was more than just a basketball game; it was also a fundraiser for Judd and Tucker, with many wonderful people showing their love and generosity. We sat in our section in the far corner of the gym. I did my best to follow through on my job as Tucker's bodyguard, but it was hard to keep his adoring fans from wanting to give a high-five to their hero.

For the national anthem, they had Tucker and his family come out to center court and introduced the young community hero. The crowd went wild. After the anthem, they played Tucker's song, "Fight Song" by Rachel Platten. As the song blasted out over the speakers, the lyrics that Tucker had adopted as his theme song rang out:

"This is my fight song, take back my life song, prove I'm all right song.
My power's turned on. Starting right now I'll be strong.
I'll play my fight song and I don't care if nobody else believes,
'Cause I've still got a lot of fight left in me."

There wasn't a dry eye in the entire gymnasium. Except Tucker's—he was smiling, soaking up the love and support, and believing every word of that song. Then he was presented with awesome gifts, including a personalized Wild jersey and tickets to a Wild game. I didn't think it could, but his smile got even bigger.

We thought Tucker would be tired and need to leave at half- time, but the energy and love from the crowd pumped him up, and he was one of the last ones to leave the gym. He went to sleep with that smile still on his face. It was definitely the right call to have him attend. This amazing event in that loving community was just as necessary as meds were.

Chapter Twenty-One

Since we were near the end of the second round of chemo, it was time to prepare for Tucker's limb replacement surgery. He would be getting a metal rod to replace his femur. During his next week in the hospital, he would get an MRI so his orthopedic surgeon could order the right "internal hardware" for his femur and knee. I was sad that Tucker needed his knee replaced, but whatever it took to make him healthy and keep him alive was totally worth it.

We went into the hospital on Martin Luther King Jr. Day, which was even worse since the other kids were home from school and having fun. Tucker, however, was on his way to his personal jail. As usual, I had to use my arm strength to keep him inside the vehicle and my heart strength to keep from crying with him. Another thing that had become "usual" was Tucker's tears stopping when he saw a homeless person at the top of the ramp. He turned to me for money and reached out his window to the cold, hungry soul. Tucker was now reminding me on Sunday nights to make sure to have a five-dollar bill ready. *How can he remember and feel other people's pain when he has so much of his own?*

Once we got to the hospital and up to the Journey Clinic, things calmed down. It is so different when you step into the world of a children's hospital. Suddenly all the children around you are also bald and hooked up to IV poles. You don't feel all alone; there are so many others going through this hell too. Later, Lisa and cousins Maggie and Amy brought great things for Tucker. One was an art project, and the other was a beautiful painting made by cousin Sophie. Sophie wrote the refrain of his/the "Fight Song" on a canvas she painted using different hues of orange. His fight song on his power color in soothing art. Such an amazing gift. It still warms my heart to look at such a work of love that honored my son so well.

The night got even better when Papa brought Kayci and Siera in for a visit, and Mark brought Hailey and Henry. Usually access-Mondays were exhausting and sad, but the A-Team was out to change that. Tucker was truly happy to see them, and not just the yummy French toast they'd brought him from Perkins. He wanted his sisters to stay the night, and the girls did too. It was so hard separating them. I tried to make Tucker laugh by reminding him that he got to stay up late but the girls had to go to bed because it was a school night, but he said he would rather be with them and at school. He meant that sincerely. I, of course, was the bad guy who had to break up the party and get the girls out the door. Judd was going to leave too, but I had him stay so that Tucker didn't have to say goodbye to everyone at once.

It also allowed me to walk the girls out to Papa's car. Kayci did a great job at being strong as she left her best friend behind. Siera couldn't fight back the tears and refused to let go of me as I tried to put her in her car seat. After five minutes of sobbing, Papa had to come help pull her arms off me so we could separate, just as I had to pull Tucker's fingers off the doorframes. Siera's pain and fear were as real and strong as Tucker's. Kayci's were too, and in many ways, hers were deeper and even more painful because she didn't let things show like Siera and Tucker did. Poor Kayci suffered in silence. I did my best to attend to the needs she wasn't showing, but never felt like I could help her enough.

That nagging feeling had been proven correct a few weeks earlier, when I told Kayci that Tucker wanted to come back into the girls' room and sleep next to her. Kayci's response left a pain in my heart that is still there today.

"You mean he does still love me?" she said very earnestly.

I fell to my knees to look her in the eyes. "What do you mean?"

With pain in her eyes, Kayci told me she thought Tucker had been sleeping in my room all this time because he didn't want to sleep next to her anymore. Oh, the agony and failure on my part to not make sure she knew what was happening. "No! Tucker has wanted to sleep next to you every night, but he had so much pain I kept him next to me to help him with that."

Kayci asked, "Are you sure?"

"Yes, honey. Tucker loves you SO much. You are his best friend! Now sleep in the lower bunk, because Tucker wants to be right next to you on the trundle bed." I got Tucker situated, and he arranged his pillows so his head could be high enough for Kayci to rub it while he fell asleep.

As soon as possible, I ran to the other side of our house and started sobbing. How had I overlooked that the sleeping arrangements needed to be explained? My poor girl was not only facing her brother's cancer, but also fearing he no longer loved her as much.

When I finally stopped crying, I went back to check on them. Kayci had fallen asleep with her hand on her best friend, and they stayed that way all night. It is so easy to fail the healthy siblings, no matter how hard one tries not to.

Chapter Twenty-Two

My next CaringBridge journal entry was on January 27. It sounded so normal, even upbeat, even though Tucker's situation had reached its new lowest point:

Hello Team Tucker,

. . . Next, we are looking at surgery on Thursday, February 4. As scary as it sounds to a nine-year-old boy, he is looking forward to getting all the black Legos out. But not half as much as his parents and entire family are. Although it won't even be the halfway point of his treatment, it will be great to not have to worry about how much more damage the tumor is doing to my poor little boy.

I am willing to bet not a single reader worried something might be wrong. To this day, I am surprised that I was able to write, sound, and act "so normal" as I wrote about the impending surgery. Because nothing was at all "normal," and there was bad news.

No one knew what I had learned seven days prior to that journal entry except Judd and Lisa, since they'd been in the same horrific meeting with the doctor the Wednesday before, and the adults of the A-Team. Everyone else would be kept in the dark until after I told Tucker. But there was no way I could tell him.

So, the surgeon had to tell him, which he did the following Wednesday, January 27. I won't always remember the date, but I will forever remember the sound of my son's bone-chilling, heart-wrenching scream.

"NOOOOOOOOOO! I AM A HOCKEY PLAYER!" Sobs followed as he fell back, covered his face, and screamed again. "NO, MOM, NO!" At this point, Judd stepped out of the room crying. Tucker's scream and the news were unbearable.

"I am so sorry, Tucker," I said, his screams still echoing in my ears.

"No, Mom! You can't let them do this!"

"I am so sorry, but like Dr. Clohisy said, this is the only way we can get rid of the pain and the black Legos."

"But I want my leg, Mom! Don't let them cut if off!"

"I promise we will get you a new, better leg. One that doesn't have any black Legos."

"But I am a hockey player, mom. They can't take my leg."

"This is how we will make you better so you can run and play sports again. I promise."

Tucker buried his head in my chest as he sobbed. My tears poured out and dripped onto his bald head. Nothing could have prepared me for how horrific it would be watching my nine-year-old son be told that his leg needed to be amputated. And nothing will ever make that memory stop hurting. The screams, the words, the sobs—I still hear them clearly. I can still see Tucker's eyebrows rise, his jaw drop, and his eyes fill with horror as Dr. Clohisy finished the sentence, and how instantly the color drained out of his cheeks. It remains a recurring nightmare for me.

I planned on telling people once Tucker knew, but Tucker made me promise not to. So, I didn't. He and I just went about our days, acting the same. Tucker acted the same at night, so while I was beside him I did too. Inside I was devastated and broken, but this news was not going to seep out; I would stay strong, stay quiet, and stay positive until there was an opportunity to explode into a million little pieces, with enough time to put myself back together again before Tucker, Kayci, or Siera noticed.

That moment didn't happen for another week. A week spent listening to Tucker's cries of pain as his knee grew so swollen the immobilizer hardly fit. A week of students and staff asking me and Tucker what the surgery would be like. A week of back-muscle spasms as it grew harder than ever to carry Tucker, since the slightest movement of his knee resulted in intense pains and loud shouts. A week of trying to get my special ed paperwork done after the kids were asleep since I was getting so behind. A week of falling asleep in tears while reliving the meeting with the doctor.

I even had to go to one of Tucker's hockey team's games. Before learning the news, he had been invited by his coach to be an assistant coach on the bench. When Tucker found out, I told him that I would tell his coach he was too tired to attend, to which he replied, "Mom, that's my team. You stay with your team. I'm going."

I said, "Sounds great!" even though it sounded horrible. So I brought him to the rink. Tucker couldn't stand, and his wheelchair didn't fit through the door to the bench, so I lifted him up and held him while the coach collapsed his wheelchair and set it up again next to the bench, where the players all had skates on their two feet and were ready to go play hockey. At that moment, however, they were all far more focused on their favorite teammate being back on the bench with them. I watched Tucker smile and chat for a few seconds but then had to run to the restroom. Not to go to the bathroom, but to cry.

Tucker stayed for the whole game and acted just like all the other kids, minus the skating and getting to play hockey. But he laughed and definitely coached. His teammates all remember his words of advice as the coach put him in charge of the whole talk before the third period. They were losing 3–0, but in the third period they scored two goals and lost 4–2. As Tucker proudly pointed out to me on the way home, the third period was the only one his teammates "won." He was sure it was due to his coaching talk. I agreed it was because of him—maybe not his talk, but definitely because of him. Those kids used Tucker's situation to be grateful for their health and for their friendship with him. Once again, young boys were giving both Tucker and me strength to continue forward.

Tuesday would be Tucker's last day of school before the surgery. I worked with the administration to make it a special day for this special boy. I was ready to schedule skywriters and bring in a three-ring circus—nothing would be too big to honor Tucker. The new executive director, Señor Perrin, had the unenviable task of telling me that wasn't the way to go. He dared to suggest that we do a small celebration at the end of the day, because perhaps Tucker was scared and didn't want that much attention about what would be the scariest day of his life. I cried when he said that. Yes, I was angry that it wouldn't be a big event, but also angry that he was absolutely correct. Tucker would be scared.

When Tuesday came, the four of us, along with all the other students and the entire staff, wore orange. Most were in the Team Tucker Go shirts that people had so generously bought and lovingly worn. It was nearly the end of the day, a day filled with lots of good wishes, a party for Tucker in his class with all forty-five third graders, and lots of support for Kayci, Siera, and me. The girls and I went to get Tucker out of his classroom. The announcement was made for everyone to go into the hallways and cheer for our hero as we sent him off and to wish him a successful surgery to get rid of his black Legos.

I wanted to cry, but soon became too filled with joy and love to have any room left for sadness. As we played his/the "Fight Song" over the intercom, Kayci pushed her best friend through the halls, with Siera carrying the sign that was made for Tucker right behind them. I took a video of the 350 people lined up along the walls cheering, waving, high-fiving, and showering my son with love. No Stanley Cup or World Series team has ever had a better parade with better fans than Tucker did for those wonderful six minutes as he went around the school twice. He truly was a hero, and that was the most amazing tribute I will ever see in my lifetime.

Chapter Twenty-Three

On Wednesday, February 3, the day before surgery, I brought Kayci and Siera to school and then went home to play hooky with Tucker. I had him choose anything he wanted to do that day. Of course, for Tucker, "anything" was severely limited. Oh how I yearned for the days where he could do anything he wanted.

Still, Tucker made a great plan. First, we went to see a movie at the theater with the comfy recliners. We had the theater to ourselves for a noon showing of *Kung Fu Panda* in 3D. Tucker grimaced and let out a groan when I had to lift him out of his chair and place him in the seat. That actually helped me to remember why surgery was so necessary. We had to get rid of my son's pain, not just the cancer. Tucker and I took some selfies of us in our cool 3D glasses, skipping school. It was wonderful laughing together and holding hands when we weren't snacking on popcorn.

The movie ended, but Tucker just sat there. I always like to watch the movie credits scroll through, but most of the time he got bored of it after a couple minutes. Not this time. Tucker sat there for all of them, and when I got up to get his chair, he didn't move. He just wanted to keep sitting there. *Could he be as sentimental as I am and want to keep soaking up the moments with me? Possible, because he is the sweetest little mama's boy.* But I didn't think that was the full story.

I reminded him we had to get going to our other venue because we needed to meet his sisters and dad after school. Then it hit me. When this day was done, there was nothing left for him to face but surgery. Nothing else to do and no other distractions. February 4 was almost here, and as we checked each activity off our list, it was that much closer.

But I couldn't let us get sad yet—we had to get to Dave & Buster's. That had become Tucker's favorite place since cancer took over our world. In there, he could still play and do nearly all of what the other kids could do. There was plenty of laughter and his new favorite game, air hockey. Tucker would stand up and use his left hand to balance him as his right hand zoomed around shooting that little plastic puck. We played and laughed. I was prepared to dump tons of money on the game card but, as often is the case, reality stopped us—Tucker was in pain standing for too long. We played other games, like Wheel of Fortune. I always loved impressing Tucker with how "brilliant" his mother was. He used to resist finishing the sentence when I would say, "Because your mother is . . ." but now he readily stated "brilliant" and flashed a smile at me.

Eventually, it was time to go meet Judd and the girls at ISLA. This time Tucker wasn't even subtle. When I started to get his coat on him, he burst into tears. "I don't want to go, Mom!" I am sure the other parents there thought my son was throwing a fit because he simply didn't want to stop playing. God, how I wished that were the case. I put down his coat, kneeled beside his wheelchair, and hugged him. "I am sorry we have to go," I softly whispered, knowing the real reason my son was so sad.

While the kids were out to eat with Judd and Grandpa

Gary, I finally revealed the horrific news I had received two weeks earlier, Tucker a week earlier, in a CaringBridge post:

It is time . . . for this tumor to get out of my son's body.

It is time . . . for Tucker to no longer be in pain, which he has been in since mid-October.

It is time . . . to stop the black Legos from trying to take my son away from me.

And the only way to do this is by amputating Tucker's leg.

I went on to explain how two weeks before, as I lay sleeping on the hospital room couch, I'd been woken up at 7:00 a.m. to have the doctor tell me that Tucker needed scans, a week earlier than planned. I'd had a horrible feeling all day that I tried to blame on being overly worried. At 2:30 p.m., we'd found out that horrible feeling was for good reason. Chemo wasn't working as well as it should, and the black Legos were not under control—the tumor had actually grown from ten centimeters to sixteen. Instead of a limb salvage operation, it would need to be an amputation.

I shared how I'd immediately been consumed with anger. The whole time I had been dragging Tucker into the hospital to have needles shoved in his chest and poison drip into his body, the damn cancer had been growing. The few tiny spots in his lungs hadn't even shrunk!

I also shared how I'd been too scared to tell the girls the news by myself, especially after hearing the visceral screams from Tucker, which were still echoing in my head. My mom and I had brought them in to meet with me and Tucker's social worker. Siera excused herself shortly thereafter to go play with Tucker in his room; however, Kayci was full of questions. I loved her first comment: "Now he will be the fastest of us on the baseball team!" (Thank you, *Dancing with the Stars,* for having amputees on the show so I could make my kids watch!)

That week was the hardest so far. So much physical and emotional pain, so many tears from all three children, so much heartbreak, all while hiding the news from everyone outside the A-Team. Even after watching videos of amputees doing sports and researching sled hockey and the Paralympics, trying to get my mind around how much life was going to change for Tucker, for all of us, was impossible. But what I readily accepted was that there was nothing I wouldn't do to get my son every experience and opportunity he desired.

That evening, the situation got even worse. Judd called from dinner to inform me that Tucker had a fever and he was bringing the kids back early. Unbelievable! The boy who hadn't had a fever yet this whole three months of chemo got one twelve hours before he could get the life-destroying tumor out of him. I quickly packed everything up for me and Tucker, and assigned my parents and Dayra at my house to receive Kayci and Siera. I rode with Tucker and Judd to the ER, and of course Lisa would meet us there. I knew she would help interpret all the factors doctors would be weighing to determine if the surgery would happen. She was also great at helping me keep Tucker as little anxious as possible. Judd stayed with us until Lisa arrived and then went home, asking me to call when I knew more.

It was a crazy night because Tucker's temperature kept fluctuating. He had a fever, then didn't, then did again. Surgery was off, then on, then really off. Lisa explained that they couldn't operate when there was a possible infection happening, which was what the fever could indicate. However, Dr. Clohisy really wanted to perform the amputation to get the cancer out as soon as possible.

After two weeks of dreading this, now I was sitting in a hospital room crossing my fingers it would happen. Fighting cancer makes up down and red blue. Nothing is ever normal.

Tucker suffered through a forty-five minute sponge bath that caused him tremendous pain at 1:45 a.m. because his fever was gone. Then his fever went up. At the 4:00 a.m. vitals there was still a chance, so my boy sobbed through another sponge bath as they washed his incredibly swollen knee. Neither Lisa nor I could do anything but hold his hands and rub his head. All of that again for his fever to come back at the 6:00 a.m. vitals. This time it was 102 degrees. No surgery, just pain and waiting while the tumor continued to grow. *Why does everything keep getting worse?*

With all this, I knew Tucker couldn't handle any more stress, so I asked for him to have continuous anti-anxiety meds administered. Besides all the drama with his vitals, he was coping with having his leg cut off. They also placed him on a morphine drip and provided his own dispenser, which helped tremendously. I was wishing I could get both of those meds too.

Tucker couldn't eat after 6:00 a.m., just in case Dr. Clohisy did decide it was safe to proceed with surgery. So, guess what Tucker's awesome Papa did? He delivered Tucker's favorite donut at 5:40 a.m. so he could enjoy a treat as we spent the day waiting to see what would happen.

After all this, I was able to see the value in the amputation. Tucker was and had been in continuous pain. I had been living with the medicine bag clutched to my body, knowing it was as essential as oxygen at that point. My family knew about Tucker's pain, but I kept many of the details of his suffering out of the public journal entries. I didn't want to bring people too far down into the sadness, so they could remain positive and optimistic. I believed that the vibe among the people surrounding him was very much felt by Tucker, so I was never going to take a chance of having that become depressing or fearful. However, there was so much work, fear, and heartache that happened in private. Looking back, I don't know how my body and mind kept up with the demands of the situation. But they did for me, and they do for cancer parents everywhere.

Chapter Twenty-Four

February 5 is a day that continues to haunt me. There have been five of them since 2016, and each one, I break down sobbing and become nearly catatonic for a while as I remember the loss of my son's leg.

But on February 5, 2016, I was much stronger. When Dr. Clohisy cleared Tucker for surgery, I smiled and told him it would be great to get rid of the pain and the black Legos. I reminded him of our research on the Paralympics and baseball players with prosthetics. I had shown him so many stories of amputees that went on to be great athletes, I had nearly cheered up myself. Yes, we had this. Tucker was still going to be a superstar athlete, but now on a whole new level of amazing.

I nearly had myself believing this amputation was a good thing, but then we arrived in the pre-op room. No sports in there, and definitely no podiums or gold medals. Just a bald little nine-year-old boy who was about to be wheeled into an operating room and leave without his right leg. Tucker had tears trickle out a few times, but I kissed them and he smiled. I was in my strong-mom bubble where only one thing existed: my child's emotional needs. At times like these, I don't have feelings, the future is not considered, the problem is distant. In this bubble there is just my smile and reassurance that everything is fine. I stayed in this zone while waiting, while suiting up to walk Tucker into the operating room, and while the sedation was administered. Calming words, loving kisses, warm smiles, and firm hand-holding.

Tucker pleasantly greeted all the nurses and then asked me to guess how many light bulbs were in the overhead light. He started counting them while I worked hard to pretend that mattered. As his eyelids started to close, I leaned down, kissed his cheek and forehead, and said, "You are amazing. You know you are my favorite boy, and I am so proud of you. You are my hero." I had said all that many times before, but never meant it as much as I did in that moment.

Tucker fell asleep. Tears started to fill my eyes, but I had one more thing to do before I could let them fall. I asked the nurse to pull back the sheet that was covering my boy's right foot. I took a picture of his sweet little toes. The ones commemorated in black ink for his footprint on his birth certificate just nine years ago. The little toes I had seen since the ultrasound pictures. The ones with "little piggies" that went to the market. I took the picture and then darted out of the operating room as the tears ran down my cheeks.

In the hall, I desperately tried to remember how to get out to the waiting room as anxiety swelled inside me. I ripped off my white gown and nearly fell over trying to get the foot coverings off. I had only a few seconds until I would implode. I needed to get to my family. I found the correct door and burst through it.

I collapsed into my mom's and sisters' arms. They literally held me. I sobbed as they lowered me onto the couch. I couldn't stand on my own; I had used all my strength for Tucker and now had none left for me.

I had just brought my son to be butchered. Those stupid

euphemistic words of "surgery" or "procedure" or even "amputation" were bullshit. My son was going to be chopped into two parts, and I'd calmly walked him in there to let it happen. That is the opposite of what a mom is supposed to do. We want to make our kids whole, not broken!

Sobbing these words elicited the responses I needed to hear. "Tucker is not being butchered," Lisa stated emphatically. "You are saving his life by getting the cancer out of him."

Sara added, "You ARE taking care of him by allowing the cancer to be taken out of him. You are an excellent mom."

I heard the words, and my brain knew they made sense. Those were the same words I had been telling myself for sixteen days since finding out the news. But my heart was still broken and couldn't understand. It wanted my son to be whole.

My phone was lighting up with texts asking about Tucker and if/when surgery would happen. I used what little strength I had to make a journal entry on CaringBridge so I didn't have to answer anyone:

The surgeon determined it was safe to operate today. Tucker was the bravest one out of all of us. He choked back tears three times and found a way to distract himself. He went in at 3:15 and fell asleep quickly as I rubbed his head and held his hand. Surgery should be over soon. May our boy keep this strength as he starts this new chapter of his life.

Obviously I didn't share what I was really feeling. It would have served no purpose to bring the focus to my feelings and my pain. All this was about Tucker—his pain, his journey, his needs, and his joy. I was merely the one lucky enough to have the ability and opportunity to take care of him. It is so hard reliving this now and admitting all the pain I kept bottled up. But if this helps even one parent feel an ounce better because they can identify with any of it, then it is worth it to keep writing.

After surgery I posted:

Surgery went well. Tucker is resting comfortably. Surgery took a couple hours and another hour before we could see him. The surgeon said the procedure went incredibly well, and they definitely got all of the tumor out. And, as he said, that is the best way to treat cancer. So now we double up on helping [Tucker] cope emotionally as well as get more chemo started within a week or two. That is too much to think about right now. For now, we will let the PICU nurses take extra good care of him and manage pain throughout the night.

Wow, I sound like my son just had a tonsillectomy. I look back now and think I was in shock. I don't remember these calm moments where I was handling things in stride. I didn't remember the night in the PICU until I read this comment. Now I remember the incredibly kind nurse who took physical care of my son and mental care of me. He was so reassuring and kept telling me how awesome Tucker was doing.

There was no sleep for me again that night in the tiny room. Judd slept on the small sofa, and I sat in a chair right next to Tucker's bed so I could hold his hand. I sat on his left side, however, still quite afraid of the right side.

What I *do* remember is an image that is permanently burned into my brain, one that continues to haunt me. In post-op, it was so hard to see the tubes, machines, and wires all over Tucker's bare chest and adorable face. The post-op nurse was on Tucker's left side, controlling the machines and explaining Tucker's current condition. I interrupted her to ask if Tucker was still asleep; when she assured me that he was, I told her I wanted to look at his leg before he woke up just in case it was hard for me to see.

The nurse said to go ahead. I placed my hand on top of the blanket where Tucker's foot should be and took a deep breath.

I pulled the blanket from that corner halfway up, and there was nothing there. I pulled it back farther and only saw a couple wires. The blanket was nearly to his waist by now—where was my son's leg? It was called an "amputation above the knee," and I was looking well past where his knee would have been.

I finally pulled up the entire blanket, and there it was: nothing! Nothing was there! There was no "leg"! There was a round little stump. There was no leg! Nothing!

I dropped the blanket and sprinted out of the room. This time I didn't make it all the way into the waiting room—I pushed open the door and yelled, "It's gone!" My sisters and Kevin ran to me as I just kept repeating the words, "It's gone! He has no leg! Lisa, it's gone! There is nothing left to put a prosthetic on! He won't be able to have a leg!"

Lisa held me and said, "Dana, it will work. They have ways of doing this. He will have a leg." Then she walked back to Tucker's post-op room with me, while Sara stayed back to support Mom, who I am sure was in hell watching me be in so much pain.

I didn't want to go look again. I leaned on Lisa physically as well as emotionally at that point. I don't think we had permission for family members to come back yet, but when her family is hurting, Lisa doesn't wait for permission. She pulled back the blanket; I could tell she was shocked too, but she hid it pretty well. She agreed, "Yes, it is very short, but the roundness is the swelling. It will get a little longer when it heals."

"Will it be long enough to put a prosthetic on it?" I asked with tears rolling down my cheeks. Lisa replied, "Most likely there will be enough of a stump to put a prosthetic leg on. But if there isn't, there is a way to put straps around the waist to attach and support the prosthesis."

What a relief. I was still horrified that Tucker only had about four inches of his leg left. Actually, it was hard to even accept it was a "leg." I was not ready for that. In that moment, it was confirmed that the bear had won the fight, as I knew he would when I dropped my son off in the woods of the operating room.

Chapter Twenty-Five

Fifteen hours after surgery, once Tucker finally believed me that it was Saturday and not still Friday, he immediately realized the Wild played that night and recited a long list of relatives he wanted to please come watch the game with him. My family was thrilled to get the invitation to come visit their hero.

Tucker definitely wasn't fully there given all the pain medicine, but it was so sweet that his essence was still coming through; he was polite and gracious, thanking people for the presents and praise. He asked how his Littles were; even in a haze, he knew he hadn't seen them for a few days and needed to check on them. Once again, Tucker had the cancer and the pain, but his thoughts were about the well-being of others. He also showered me with concern and love, repeating, "I love you, Mommy," over and over. Each time was an injection of joy; it was like he knew my heart was shattered and that each "I love you" glued a little piece back on.

Sunday afternoon, Tucker was able to sit up at the side of the bed. It was wonderful to see him upright. He was exhausted and scared of how to manage this, but the amazing boy found the courage to do so anyway. Tucker made sure to always be covered up with blankets, and I noticed he never looked down toward his legs, or leg. He was thrilled to see his sisters and Helstrom cousins come visit him that afternoon. Dr. Clohisy made a special point to come to the hospital on his day off to visit as well. He was very impressed with how well Tucker was dealing with the pain and situation as a whole. Tucker really made an impression on Dr. Clohisy and the entire wonderful staff at U of M Masonic.

While Tucker was busy with the Helstroms, I was able to spend much of the day out in the hall making secret arrangements. I had gotten a text on Saturday from my friend Jaci, who was my former and Judd's current neighbor. It turned out her coworker, Brittney, was the best friend of Carly, Jason Zucker's fiancé. Apparently, Carly had told Brittney how Jason met this amazing little boy during his visit to Masonic in December and still talked about him. Brittney had figured out that the "boy" was the same one Jaci was connected to. Upon learning Tucker would be getting his leg amputated, Jaci had started working on a plan to help cheer up Tucker.

Once Jaci and Brittney had it arranged, they let me in on the secret: Jason wanted to come visit Tucker! Jaci had only asked for a hockey stick or jersey that she could deliver, but once Jason heard there was a way for him to reconnect with Tucker, he insisted he deliver gifts personally. I was shocked to tears and couldn't believe I was now texting Carly and finalizing a time for them to come see Tucker.

Finally, everything was set. Sunday evening, I could tell Tucker the news. "Tucker, the best person you can imagine is coming to visit you tomorrow. Guess who it is!"

"Jack?" Tucker responded in a quiet voice, mind still hazy from the morphine.

"No, I am talking about a famous person."

Tucker's eyes opened bigger than I had seen them in two days. "A hockey player?"

"Yep!" I answered.

Tucker optimistically questioned, "Jason Zucker?!"

"YES!" I can still see his huge smile in my mind right now. *What a relief, my son will be happy again.* I had been wondering for days. It was so wonderful to finally have some good news to give to Tucker. He smiled the rest of the night, healing both his body and his mind a little quicker.

Monday was full of excitement. Around 1:00 p.m., only sixty-six hours after Tucker had his leg amputated to the upper thigh, Judd and I watched as Lisa and his PT, Erin, used their gifts of persuasion and encouragement to convince him he could walk. I thought this was crazy soon, and so did Tucker, but apparently it improves recovery time dramatically to start moving again. Lisa and Erin agreed Tucker was strong enough to do this, so they worked together setting up the walker and teaching Tucker how to move his new body. He had to learn how to steady himself, balance, use his arm strength, and move the walker and his left foot.

I could see the fear in Tucker's eyes and even a couple tears as he sat on the side of the bed and placed his hands on the walker. I wanted to run across the room and pick him up and walk for him. Tucker would have sat there worrying and contemplating for a long time, but Lisa knew that wouldn't help matters. She and Erin gave specific instructions and reassured him they would *not* let him fall. He stood up, steadied himself, and took that first step, which was pivoting back and forth on his foot. With that, his look of fear was replaced with cautious optimism, and he took a second step. At that point he was filled with determination and "walked" six more feet to the recliner, then sat down.

When Tucker learned to walk on the evening of his first birthday, I never thought I would again be standing a few feet away, nervously watching as my son took his "first steps." This was even more exciting, and once again I cheered. This time, it was enough to cause tears. I told Tucker they were tears of joy, but that was only half true. Half of them were tears of devastation as I watched my son step into a scary new world with fewer possibilities and greater limitations.

Tucker was *so* strong and *so* determined to get this accomplished. He told me privately that he wanted to walk because Jason Zucker was coming in a few hours—he wanted to show Jason that he was strong and didn't need to be lying in a bed. My son definitely set goals for himself and then worked hard to meet them. I was so proud of this kid.

At six o'clock, February 8, Jason Zucker and Carly Aplin entered Tucker's room. This time, instead of wearing his Wild jersey, Jason was wearing very stylish clothes and a scarf around his neck tied just so. Instead of looking like a professional athlete, he looked like a professional model. Carly could also have been a model with her beautiful face and long, flowing blonde hair. I was even more nervous now, as they seemed even more like celebrities. Jason presented Tucker with two amazing gifts: a Wild jersey that had been signed by all the players that morning at the team practice, and one of Jason's own hockey sticks. He showed Tucker the markings he put on each stick. This one was number 53—Jason numbers all his sticks during the season. On each one, he writes "Mom & Dad" and the initials of his best friend, who died when they were teenagers. His parents definitely raised an incredibly kind-hearted young man.

Tucker was so in awe that he was actually quiet. My son

was never speechless, until now, as he was still in disbelief that he got to hang out with his sports hero. But then he got over it, and when I was getting ready to thank Jason and Carly and let them be on their way, Tucker asked Jason if he wanted to play Xbox with him.

Ugh, I thought, *I don't know if that is what Jason had in mind.* I interjected and told Tucker I was sure they were busy and couldn't stay. Jason immediately spoke up and said he absolutely wanted to stay and play with Tucker. I started to tell him he didn't have to when Carly laughed and reassured us that Jason wasn't just staying to be nice—he loved playing video games and hadn't had the chance since moving out of his place with Charlie Coyle (his best friend and a center on the Wild) and in with her and her daughter, Sophia.

Jason proceeded to take off his coat, which revealed the Team Tucker Go shirt Tucker had given him the day they met back in December. Wow! Now he was a professional athlete, a great-looking model, *and* a total sweetheart. He pulled his chair right up next to Tucker's recliner. The two proceeded to talk and laugh like old friends. Jason and Carly ended up staying for two hours, time that was filled with joking, laughter, and even teasing each other. Tucker and Zucker looked and sounded like buddies.

As I walked Jason and Carly to the elevator, I told Jason he could not possibly realize how much this meant to Tucker. He said he loved it and told me to let Carly know the next time Tucker was in for chemo. Again I was shocked. *How is a twenty-four-year-old professional athlete this sweet and generous?* I told Jason he had done enough, but they made me promise to keep in touch and said they would definitely be back to hang out with Tucker again. Amazing. It would be years later that I would fully understand that Jason truly did have a deep and lasting connection with Tucker. They have so much in common: a love for hockey, for family, and for helping others.

Even with a celebrity appearance and an incredibly fun evening, Tucker remembered what was most important to him and begged to have his sisters spend the night with him. I was thrilled to say yes. Being late to school is not a big deal in the scheme of things. I put the air mattress down right next to Tucker's bed, my heart full as I watched the three of them fall asleep, together. I didn't think I could be happy so soon after the amputation. I knew hard times were ahead, but I welcomed the joy and let it fill my body.

On Tuesday, only four days after the amputation, Tucker made even bigger strides, literally. During his morning PT session, he decided, on his own, to pass the recliner and go all the way over to the couch. Dr. Clohisy once again stopped by personally to check on him. The two chatted, and then Tucker allowed him to take the dressing off his "leg." Tucker had not yet looked under the covers, and every time I used the urinal bottle, he looked away. Given my reaction when I'd first seen it, I was very supportive of Tucker not looking until he felt ready to do so. But Dr. Clohisy was not only excellent in the operating room, he was equally as excellent bedside. His calming, matter-of-fact approach and kid-friendly words were so effective, Tucker decided to look at what was left of his right leg.

I held my breath waiting for Tucker's reaction, ready to comfort him when he saw the stump. But my boy stayed calm, and there were no tears. In my eyes there were, but I held them back. As Tucker looked for a few seconds, then looked back to the doctor and kept chatting, I found another level of pride and an expanse of how impressed I was with this amazing boy who I was so fortunate to have call me "Mom."

Tucker's hard work with moving, eating, and staying positive had the desired effects of helping his body recover. He was actually discharged on Wednesday, only five days after a very major amputation. Dr. Clohisy remarked that this was the quickest recovery and discharge after a leg amputation he could remember. If Tucker hadn't been everybody's hero yet, he sure was by this point.

Maybe that is why this happened to Tucker and me. Apparently, we were supposed to be an example of how to approach, battle, and overcome cancer for all to see and admire. I can't express how much I wished it didn't have to be us doing this. But I didn't get a choice, so there was nothing left to do but rise to the challenge and beat this.

Tucker was excited to be discharged, but worried about how he was going to continue hiding under blankets so no one could see that he only had one leg. It was then that I told Tucker that when I'd dropped off his sisters at school that morning, I'd gone into his classroom to talk with his classmates. Tucker's first reaction was anger—"MOM! I told you not to tell anyone!"

"I know, honey, and I didn't until the day of your surgery. But I had to tell people, first of all because everyone cares about what happens to you, and second because there was no way they weren't going to notice," I explained.

"What did you tell my friends?" Tucker asked nervously.

"I told them that because there were so many black Legos in your leg, it had to be removed so you could get rid of cancer.

I explained how right now there is no leg, but soon you'll have a fake one, called a prosthetic."

Tucker looked down and was quiet as I held his hand and rubbed his back. He was afraid of the next question he had: "Did they ask if I look weird?"

It was wonderful to tell him that when I told the kids they would notice that his pant leg was flat and only see one shoe, not one single kid laughed or even smiled. They cried out, "How is he doing?" "Is he sad?" "Tell him we want him to come back to school right away!" Then the best comment: "Tell him it isn't funny when he isn't here, so hurry back so he can tell us his jokes and make us laugh."

His shoulders relaxed, and a smile slowly emerged. "Did they really say that, Mom?"

"Oh my gosh, yes! They miss you so much! They don't care how many legs you have. They want their friend back. In fact, I think the only problem you will have is them fighting over who gets to help you. They already started arguing about who gets to eat lunch with you first and push your wheelchair. Señora Shrestha had to start a new lottery system because the kids in the other third-grade classroom were demanding they get to skip lunch and recess and hang out with you in your 'office' too!"

Tucker was beaming. He loved his classmates and was excited to hear how much they loved him back. These kids were amazing. They inspired me and helped me as much as they helped Tucker.

Chapter Twenty-Six

Going home was always joyous, especially after this long stay of one full week. This time, however, bigger challenges awaited us. Tucker needed to learn how to get around our house, take many new oral medications, and get into bed and onto the couch comfortably, along with the obvious task of learning how to live with one leg. But right away we noticed one thing was better: for the first time in three months, Tucker could face forward in the car. Since October, he'd had to sit sideways across the bench seating with his pained knee up and across the seats. Even better, it was the first ride in weeks with no screams, not even when there was a big bump.

Once we got home, we were pleasantly surprised to see that our house had been completely cleaned and reorganized. Leave it to the A-Team to make sure everything was as ready as it could be for this transition. While "A-Team" started as a nickname, it came to represent our actions and our philosophy of family. We are a team working together to ensure each other's happiness and well-being. There is no time, no distance, no hour of the day or night that we won't be there to support whomever of us is in need. Obviously, during Tucker's war with cancer it was my family of four that was in need, and it was the other eighteen who gave tirelessly.

Tucker had to stay home from school the first day, so of course Grandma was there to take care of him. I was nervous to leave him, but I was so behind at work and my students needed me too, so I went. It was also necessary for me to be at ISLA when I could because I had no accrued "sick days" like teachers in public school districts do. I will admit I was very jealous Judd had nearly one hundred days banked, so he never had to worry about loss of income. ISLA is a charter school, so I didn't have that financial security after my nine sick days were used. My amazing coworkers had each donated one of their sick days to me, but those had already run out too since Tucker and I were in the hospital so much. It was hard to see my paychecks in the amount of $167 every two weeks, but I was being supported by donations from many loving and generous people. I was so grateful for the financial support, because it was not an option for me to not be by Tucker's side. I couldn't have kept my house or the girls' sports without the community's help.

I texted my mom throughout the morning to check on how things were going. Grandma was getting Tucker to eat some pancakes and was even happy to let him watch SpongeBob. We both thought things were going well, but then I got the call. When it wasn't a text, that meant it was urgent.

I darted out of a meeting and answered. I could barely hear my mom say, "I can't get him to calm down!"

Drowning out her words was Tucker wailing and screaming. I yelled into the phone, "Did he fall? Is he in pain?"

Mom tried to stay calm, but I could hear anxiety in her voice. "No. He wants his leg back."

I told my principal I had to leave and raced out the door. There was no point calling and talking while I drove home because I knew those screams meant Tucker was in an intense panic attack. Thankfully, the house was only ten minutes away, so I was soon running inside and holding Tucker's hand.

He was still screaming for his leg. His eyes were red, and his cheeks were soaked with tears. I hugged him, squeezing tightly in an attempt to squelch his shaking.

"Mommy's here, Tucker. Mommy's here." I wanted to whisper it softly into his ear like I had for every bad dream, injury, and fearful moment of his life. But he couldn't hear me, so I was saying it loudly and holding him tightly while Grandma held his hand. After a few minutes, Tucker stopped screaming and shaking and crumpled into my arms. "Mom, where is my leg? I want it, Mommy. I want my leg!" he sobbed.

"Honey, it was full of black Legos. We wanted to get rid of it so you can get a new one that is healthy." I looked him in the eyes as I held his sweet cheeks, trying to dry them. "I promise you, we will get you a better leg. It is just going to take a little while."

I got up from kneeling on the floor and sat next to him so he could lay his head on my chest. Sitting there, I could now see my mom, who was on the other side of Tucker, still holding his hand. She is so incredibly strong, especially when it comes to hiding fear. But this was too much for even her to block out. Her eyes were filled with pain, her body rigid. It is extremely rare for my mom to be helpless, even more rare for her to not be able to relieve a grandchild of pain.

I reassured her and Tucker that everything was going to be OK, then told them a work story for distraction. I was astounded and proud that I was the one reassuring my mom. This was the first time in my life it wasn't the other way around. I had arrived at the level of my mom's parenting, able to take care of everyone. My pride in myself had never been higher.

Chapter Twenty-Seven

No one expected Tucker to go to school seven days after a major amputation, not even me. But Thursday night, as I asked him who he wanted to stay home with him, he replied, "No one. I am going to school."

I was thrilled—I wanted him near me so I could take care of him—but I wanted to make sure he was emotionally ready for this first time in public. So that night, while lying next to him, I double-checked and asked if he was sure. I am so glad I did, because I loved his answer. "Yes, Mom, I want to go to school. I missed you too much today."

Tucker and I were always close, but going through this hell together had made our bond even stronger. I responded, "Good, because I missed you today too, buddy."

I could tell Tucker was anxious about going into school. Three times he ensured the blanket was covering his "legs"; he told me he didn't think he was going to take the blanket off all day. I reassured him that he was in charge of that decision and there was no hurry. As I wheeled him into his classroom, his friends/classmates were taking a group picture. Tucker shouted, "Wait for me!"

The kids squealed with delight at seeing their friend and quickly made room for his chair in the middle of the group, then surrounded him for the picture. In less than the full minute I'd predicted it would take, Tucker had reacclimated to the classroom. His classmates were *so* happy to see him, and Tucker's smile spread across his entire face. He was thrilled to be back with his friends, his teachers, his sisters, and the entire ISLA community. It was his second family.

At ten o'clock that morning there was a school assembly; all 300 students would be there. I knew it was best for Señora Shrestha to take Tucker, since it was a class activity. I made sure to be in the hallway, though, in case he gave me a look that told me to come help. He did look at me as he rolled by with his blanket perfectly covering his entire lower body; there was some fear in his eyes, but not enough for me to step in. I smiled and gave him a thumbs-up.

During the assembly, I forced myself to stay at least thirty feet away from Tucker. I knew I would run to take him out of there in case this was too much for him, but I wouldn't go over there unless that happened. It didn't. About twenty minutes into the assembly, I saw Tucker discreetly take the blanket off his lap. I hurried over there to check in with him. "Tucker, do you want your blanket off? Are you sure?"

He replied, "Yes, Mom, it's really hot in here."

I accepted that answer and leaned in to whisper, "I am so proud of you!" I knew, as did he, that the real reason was the acceptance and love he felt gave him the strength to stop hiding his new body.

After the assembly, I made it a whole half hour before I walked by Tucker's classroom to check on him. I quickly scanned the room and found his wheelchair—but it was *empty*! I had to come in and check it out. There was Tucker, lying on the rug making a poster with his classmates. My heart just about burst with happiness, pride, and love. I left before anyone saw a tear roll down my cheek.

Tucker went on to enjoy his personal recess and lunch with a friend. After lunch, it was time for the Friendship Party, ISLA's wonderful version of Valentine's Day. Tucker participated in all the games and activities excitedly. I knew the room parents had modified the games last night when I told them Tucker would be coming to make sure he could fully participate. That was one of a million times that the community took the extra time and effort to accommodate my son, to allow him to be just like all the other kids. The benefits and joy of those efforts can never be measured.

Chapter Twenty-Eight

I will forever remember every single detail of the amazing day that was Saturday, February 13, 2016.

I will begin by saying that every Minnesotan should be incredibly proud of the entire Minnesota Wild hockey organization. They are wonderful, kind people who care about their fans and community. With the help of Jason Zucker, assistant coach Darby Hendrickson, and Andrew Heydt, the director of team operations and player relations, Tucker had the single most exciting day of his life. So many dreams were filled; so many heroes turned into acquaintances; and so much joy washed away thoughts of cancer, chemo, and even his missing leg. Tucker's mind and heart were completely filled with excitement, friendship, and love for his team, the Wild.

I think the plan was put into motion that Wednesday. That was the day when Aaron Holm came to visit Tucker. Aaron is the creator of Wiggle Your Toes foundation, which helps amputees make the transition of losing a limb and adjusting to prosthetics. At the end of his visit, he mentioned something about "making a call" when Tucker told him he was going to the Wild game on Saturday with his friends Charlie and Greyson. Jason Zucker had also mentioned checking into something for Tucker during his visit. Tucker and I were just excited to be going to the game and watching from a suite; we didn't think it could get any better.

But it could. And did! Thanks to Aaron and Darby, Tucker was invited to watch the pregame warm-ups from the Wild bench! I think I screamed louder than Tucker did when we found out. Then, on Friday night, I received a call from Andrew. I couldn't believe the Wild was calling me! As my parents laughed at my inability to speak, Andrew confirmed the details of Tucker being on the Wild bench for pregame, but then he had more news for me. He said, "Yes, we are planning on having Tucker join us for pregame, but most of his fun will happen after the game."

I was confused and flustered. What could be more fun than pregame on the bench, during which I am sure his hero Jason would give him a fist bump and he would see the other players of his favorite team, or afterward, when he would watch the game in a suite with his buddies? Seriously, what could be better than all that?

Having Jason Zucker bring Tucker into the locker room after the game to meet all the players. That's what!

I wanted to scream, but it was 9:30 p.m. and the girls were asleep, so I couldn't. I hurried into my room, where Tucker was playing on his phone in my bed. I was hyperventilating, but caught my breath enough to say, "Tucker, guess what you get to do tomorrow."

With a huge grin on his face, Tucker responded, "I know, sit on the bench for pregame," remaining calm and not even looking up from *Subway Surfer*.

"Yes, but something even better!"

My awesome son nonchalantly answered, "They want me to skate with them?" with a twinkle in his eyes.

How does he do that? How can he tell jokes one week after his leg was cut off and he will never skate again? Whenever I think I am strong, I get reminded that Tucker is even stronger. I fought back the tears and tried to be funny too. "Nope, honey. The Wild did not draft you."

"Darn, I thought I was pretty good!" Tucker instantly quipped back.

"You are awesome. But the other surprise"—I couldn't wait a second longer, no more jokes—"is that you have been invited to go into the locker room with Jason after the game and meet the rest of the players."

". . ." Nothing. Tucker could not find words. His face turned bright red as he fell back onto his pillow and then put his blanket over his face. My son was nearly levitating from the bliss that was consuming him. I sat there and soaked in the visual. Joy—my son was filled with joy. I had worried how long it would be before he was truly happy again. Thanks to Jason, Aaron, Darby, and Andrew, I didn't have to wait very long at all.

The next day, Greyson and Charlie and their dads Bob and Chris picked us up. These two boys were Tucker's best baseball and hockey friends, and their dads were the boys' baseball coaches and now family friends. The boys were sweet, balancing being extra kind to Tucker (taking turns pushing his wheelchair and making sure he got everything first) with treating him the same by joking and teasing him about girls.

Then we parked. Well, *we* didn't park. Rather, we pulled into the players' underground parking lot and security personnel parked Chris's car. Tucker was Big Time now, and the five of us were thrilled to be his entourage. Next, we went through the belly of the Xcel Energy Center, up to the suites, as I sent a text to the Wild front office staff, as one does, to let them know we were ready for our appearance on the players' bench.

I wish I could put into words how Tucker felt, but he couldn't explain it. For me, I can say it was the first time I have ever been starstruck. My heart was racing as we stood by the locker room door and twenty amazing athletes filed past us. It was all surreal. Then we went down the players' corridor to the rink. There were a couple stairs to get up to the bench, so I carried Tucker from his wheelchair up the steps. This yanked me out of my bliss back into our crappy reality, but thirty seconds later, when Jason skated over to chat with Tucker, I was happy once again. We were there for about fifteen minutes, all of it exhilarating, as one after another the guys came over to fist-bump Tucker, give him a puck, and/or ask him how he was doing. Jason checked on Tucker every couple minutes, in between his warm-upshots and the visits of the other players.

I was shocked. These were supposed to be sports stars, not real men with big hearts who genuinely cared about a boy who'd lost his leg to cancer. But that is exactly what happened—those men showed Tucker that he was as important as the warm-up. And Tucker felt it. His joy was palpable and only exceeded by his self-worth. These heroes of his were proud to meet him, little nine-year-old Tucker. They didn't care that he was missing a leg; in fact, they thought he was a hero because of it. I was watching these men re-instill Tucker's self-pride, and for that I will never be able to repay them.

In the suite, Tucker was having so much fun with the boys, but cancer always makes sure its presence is known and felt. Twice he had tears from the pain, and once he had to crawl up the stairs because his left leg was too tired to hop. When the time came for the national anthem, he couldn't stand up. *Damn cancer, it can't leave us alone for even a few hours.* I gave Tucker his next dose of oxycodone; when Charlie and Greyson saw him cry, they patted him on the back. With that, Tucker wiped away his tears, and about five minutes later started cheering. The five of us followed his lead and also tried to erase cancer from our minds and our afternoon.

When the game ended, the six of us headed down to the "Arena" level (people need permission to get down there!). Andrew was waiting for us along with Aaron and his wife, Amanda, who is actually a high school friend of mine. The excitement built as we were led to the locker room. There was Tucker's hero, Jason Zucker, standing outside the door waiting for him. A little of my excitement faded when I found out I would have to wait outside, a gender thing. But I was happy as I watched three awestruck boys get led inside, one having his wheelchair pushed by his sports hero.

The boys didn't come out for over a half hour. Who knew Tucker would have a lot to chat about with his favorite sports team ever?! When they finally emerged, all three of them had perma-grins plastered across their faces. They had just experienced something they would never forget.

Chapter Twenty-Nine

Tucker had more wonderful hockey events to enjoy during his week before returning to the hospital to start chemotherapy once again. The following Saturday, he was treated to an outpouring of community love by the Hopkins Youth Hockey Association. They dedicated the Mite Jamboree to Tucker and created a celebration of support for him, Kayci, Siera, and me. I loved the entire event, especially wheeling Tucker onto the ice with his teammates and looking up to the stands and hallways crowded with people all wearing orange and Team Tucker Go shirts. We greeted all the people from our community and beyond who came to show their support for the four of us. I was beyond touched to also have old friends from near and far coming to meet my kids and give me a supportive hug.

Tucker's exhausting but fun day continued—together with his dad, grandpa, and uncle Jeff, he headed off to watch the North Star/Wild Alumni game at the TCF Bank outdoor stadium. Even exhaustion and the cold couldn't keep him away from an amazing hockey event like that. The gang had a wonderful time with the tickets that Tucker had been given by his CFL therapist the day before.

Sunday, Tucker was back in the cold again, this time watching his favorite team. One of his hockey coaches was able to get us tickets to the first ever outdoor NHL game in Minnesota. It was a very cold day, which is extra challenging when a child is immobile and in a wheelchair. The game was awesome. The Wild played out of their minds and demolished the Chicago Blackhawks 6 to 1. All the scoring was helpful, as it caused all of us to get to our feet and cheer (or in Tucker's case, get to his foot).

After the fourth goal, I was standing next to Tucker when he said, "Look, Mom, I'm clapping."

I didn't catch what he was saying and answered, "I know, isn't this awesome?!"

He repeated it again: "Mom, look, I'm clapping."

I stopped cheering and watched Tucker clap. He was using two hands to clap. He was standing and using both hands. That meant he was not holding the railing. Tucker was balancing on his left foot for the first time!

I could think of no better venue nor motivation for this first. I saw not only pride in Tucker's eyes, but also hope. My telling him for weeks that the amputation wouldn't stop him had just been words from a doting mother. At this moment, he could start to believe them. I wanted to hug him, but I didn't want to ruin his balance. Also, I could tell he just wanted to be like everyone else, standing and clapping. It was an amazing moment that I will forever cherish.

For Tucker, the fun ended before the game did. During the third period, Zucker got knocked down hard and his head hit the ice. Tucker was the first to see it and yelled, "That's Jason!" He was a wreck as they helped Jason skate to the locker room. He anxiously watched for Zucker to return to the bench, but he didn't. Tucker couldn't even focus on the rest of the game and begged me to text Carly to see if Jason was OK. I resisted at first, but I knew Tucker was very distraught. Carly was nice enough to answer my text right away and reported that Jason was fine; they just had to be safe in case there was a concussion. Tucker was minimally relieved and stayed quiet the last five minutes of the game. This boy had so much empathy.

Chapter Thirty

The two-week respite from the hospital—befriending Jason Zucker and the Wild, spending time with family, friends, and classmates—was like being on a rocket ship headed to Tucker's favorite planet, Saturn. Now it was time for re-entry on planet Cancer. I feared the rocket would catch on fire and wondered how I would extinguish it before the burns got too severe. All three kids were quiet that night, Tucker most of all. When Kayci asked him what was wrong, he told her that he was worried about Jason. He was, but I knew he was worrying about himself as well.

I was sure Tucker was remembering how two days earlier, on Friday at the hospital, Dr. Weigel had asked me to meet with her after his appointments were done. I'd called Lisa, who of course had rearranged her work schedule to come be by my side. It wasn't good news.

The scan had shown that seven to eight spots that were there two months ago had persisted. Dr. Weigel said that these results showed that the regimen was just keeping the cancer "at bay," and therefore she needed to move Tucker onto a different protocol. She'd started to explain "Plan B" to me, but I'd reminded her that Tucker worried when I met with doctors privately, so I needed to hurry back to him. Soon enough I would know how much damage this next "cure" would cause. I could wait.

When I'd returned, Tucker had immediately asked me,

"What did Dr. Weigel say?" with a voice and body full of anxiety. I'd continued my approach of shielding him from as much of the bad news for as long as possible; to answer his question, I told Tucker that she wanted to let me know that the scan showed there was one 1x1 black Lego left in his lungs. Even with this very toned-down version of the scan results, Tucker had been absolutely devastated. He'd lain back in silence, fighting back tears. As I'd continued and explained that I had no doubt that we would get that last one out, he had remained silent. Thankfully, he was distracted by his sisters and TV once we got home from the hospital.

As I'd anticipated, Monday morning was hell. Tucker cried the entire morning, yelling, "I want to go to school!" Of course he did—that was where kids were laughing, playing, learning interesting things, and then going home. At the hospital, kids were sick, bored, learned about medicines, experienced horrible side effects, and couldn't go home.

That day, I learned that Plan B was what Dr. Weigel called the "heavy artillery." I clarified, "We have a small town, but we're bringing in the bomb that could take out a whole city?" She concurred.

"Supercharged T" is what Tucker named this new poison, which children with cancer have to settle for as "medicine." He would be admitted on Mondays and get supercharged T each night for five straight hours while flushing it with fluids. It was so sad for Tucker, Kayci, Siera, and me to find out that hospital stays would now last two days longer. I assured the kids that we would at least have fifteen days at home before the next round. What I didn't share with them was that Tucker would be home this long because this chemo was so hard on a body that it needed that much time to recover. This one would wipe out Tucker's blood cells, causing him to be exhausted and need transfusions.

Monday night after Tucker fell asleep, I will admit I felt hopeless. I had been fighting a gut feeling ever since the January scans—Tucker wasn't going to beat this. I *never* admitted this feeling to anyone; I felt that I was a horrible mom for even having it. I acted positive and hopeful for Tucker, Kayci, and Siera, but that night I was feeling defeated and losing hope. I was dreading restarting this horrific battle just as badly as Tucker was. I didn't want to peel my son's fingers off the doorframes ever again, to be deafened by his screams as I carried him to the car and forced him inside. I didn't want to return to the evenings of sobs when his visitors left. *Why didn't Plan A work? Why did my son have to get his leg cut off?* I had stayed positive, we had done all the right things, and still this beast was actively trying to devour my son. I could have cried all night, but I was distracted by the dozen times I had to help my son pee out poison into a urinal bottle.

Thankfully, I felt better on Tuesday—it was needed, because Tucker had a hard week. He shed tears every day and had anxiety attacks every night. He was being mentally tortured by being locked inside this prison, trapped inside a body that wouldn't let him walk or run, let alone skate. He missed his classmates, his friends, his cousins, and especially his sisters. Wednesday he woke up crying, asking me why the black Legos had to come to his body; then he went on to cry about not getting to play in the pros. Tears fell like rain. I let him cry for a while and wholeheartedly agreed it was unfair. But then it was time for me to be positive and tell him the possibilities.

Luckily, I was raised in a sports-loving family, headed by my grandma's passion for great teams and great athletes. Thus, I knew exactly who to talk about with Tucker: Jim Abbott. This was the man who not only won a gold medal for the US Olympic baseball team, but also got a no-hitter when he pitched for the Yankees, all while only having one hand. This dried up Tucker's tears and opened his mind to dreaming once again about professional sports. I told him he could be the first major league ball player with an artificial limb if that was what he wanted to do. I assured him that he could have dreams, and I would make sure he had everything he needed to achieve them. "Remember, there's nothing we can't do."

On these bad weeks, I was sure to get Tucker as much professional support as possible. I had the music therapist come see him; she had Native American flutes and drums, which Tucker had loved ever since our vacation to South Dakota. I bought him his very own flute, and the two of them played duets together. It was beautiful to see and hear. I also had a chaplain visit with Tucker and me. It was very welcoming that she did not mind our lack of religious practice—she was respectful, calming, and helpful as she talked to us a couple times each week we were there. I also asked the integrative medicine therapist to meet with me and Tucker. She taught us many techniques to add to the ones we were already using for Tucker's anxiety. Of course, I continued to be his social secretary and schedule at least one visitor per evening. I was even able to find someone to come during the day: his friend Gregory, who was homeschooled. Their time together was very beneficial for both of them.

Friday night, I didn't need sports stories to cheer up Tucker; Kayci and Siera did that for me. He had been asking all week for his sisters to be able to stay overnight, and finally it was time. He and Kayci painted together over at the table while Siera turned his hospital bed into a gymnastics mat and headstand center. Then there was the loudness of pajama time, and of course the argument of who got to sleep next to Mom, as the air mattress was next to the couch. As I predicted, Kayci bowed out of the argument as soon as she realized that the other side of the air mattress was closer to Tucker. The noise and arguing didn't bother Tucker; in fact, I think it helped him relax.

I was with all three of my children, and all of them were happy. There is nothing greater.

Chapter Thirty-One

Cancer brings lots of surprises, nearly all of them bad ones. However, we were pleasantly surprised at how Tucker's first week at home went after his first week of the supercharged T. On Monday, Tucker's blood counts were surprisingly good, so he hurried into school and participated in everything, including physical education class at the end of the day. He'd had to miss phys ed class for four months because of the potential damage it could have done to his leg; that was no longer an issue. Tucker participated in all of it. He did the warm-ups just like the others: laps (with his walker), push-ups (with his newly acquired arm muscles), the mini-trampoline (on his left leg with a friend's support), and jumping jacks (I am not even sure how)! What? It was so amazing and wonderful to watch. Then I got to watch as Tucker's face glowed in delight and pride as he shared the story of his gym class with everyone at family dinner.

Tucker felt great again on Tuesday, so there was another day of school and then Grandma/Papa-care for the evening. Tucker was quite happy to show us all how he could now stand for four straight minutes on his one leg. The rest of us tried, and no one got past a minute.

Wednesday afternoon, I could see that Tucker was tired. He turned down the option to play with Jayden and went to bed early that night. I brought him to his labs the following morning so I could be there to console him if the numbers were bad.

They were, and I had to bring him home for the day. Tucker broke into tears, but I will admit I was relieved. When the "supercharged T" wasn't slowing him down, I was *very* nervous that my son was some type of cockroach to chemotherapy. I was worried that if it wasn't hurting the good parts, it might not be hurting the bad parts, like the first protocol. I had been terrified during the labs, but kept it well hidden. It is mind-boggling how cancer can make a mom wish for her child to be sick. Cancer makes everything wrong.

By Saturday, Tucker was well enough to get back to his job as assistant hockey coach, then head up to Judd's house, where he told his dad he wanted to play catch and pass the hockey puck. It was Tucker's first time using a hockey stick since October, but he quickly figured out how to pass back and forth with his dad and Jack. He also mastered catching and even throwing the baseball.

Instead of being content with his new skills and increased sports activity, however, Tucker wanted to do more. I will never forget my shock, and joy, when Judd sent me a video of Tucker rollerblading. Tucker used his walker and the rollerblade on his left foot to skate down the sidewalk. All his St. Michael friends loved having him outside playing sports with them once again. Just like his other friends, they seamlessly made modifications to the game and included Tucker as fully as they always had. So many little heroes in this journey.

Tucker's weekend managed to get even better Sunday night. Once again, Andrew Heydt gave Tucker tickets to a Wild game. I let Carly know that Tucker would be at the game, and of course she told us Jason wanted to see him afterward. We started to head down to the front rows, where Jason and the other players were talking; when we were stopped by the Xcel Center security, I explained that this was Tucker, a friend of Jason Zucker, and we were allowed to pass. Tucker couldn't have been prouder.

I started to get in position to carry Tucker down the stairs, with my brother Mark helping me figure out the best way to do so. There were about sixty steps, and I was worried how long I would last. Suddenly, Tucker put his arm over the railing, lifted up his foot, and slid down the railing on his armpit! This crazy kid could figure out so much. We all laughed as we hurried to catch up with him.

Once down with the players, Tucker chatted with Ryan Suter and Charlie Coyle about the game as only he could. Suter and Tucker connected on their love of playing defense and even ripped Zucker a little. It was amazing to watch my son hang out with professional hockey players so effortlessly and to see their true enjoyment.

Eventually it was time to get going. As the players left, Tucker was thrilled to watch the sports news team get set to start an interview right there on the Wild bench. The sportscaster said hi to Tucker and asked him about the Wild. Tucker's response blew him away. The man they were about to interview had just arrived, so the sportscaster gave Tucker another question: "Do you know who this guy is?"

Tucker answered, "Of course, that's the assistant coach Darby Hendrickson."

The sportscaster got an idea. "Tucker, how would you like to introduce Darby on the news?"

Tucker's eyes lit up! He hopped down the last two steps and stood next to the sportscaster. The cameraman pointed, and

Tucker did his thing, introducing with flair "Darr-by HEN-drick-son!"

After they chatted a few seconds, Tucker said goodnight to the viewers. As Tucker hopped out of the camera's view, Darby interrupted his interview to talk briefly about how amazing Tucker was and how the whole Wild team drew inspiration from him. Wow, them too?

Chapter Thirty-Two

Despite Tucker's great physical progress, his emotional health continued to suffer. As a mother, it was heartbreaking to hear his cries, endure his screams, and feel his suffering. Thankfully, as a mental health practitioner I cognitively understood that all this was healthy, part of the grieving process for the body and lifestyle he'd once had. However, I also knew when the symptoms were too severe and needed medical intervention. That point had come. I had tried every alternative intervention to no avail. So, during Tucker's most recent hospitalization, I asked for him to be seen by the psychiatrist.

The first answer I received was that there was an opening in a few weeks. I responded, "That doesn't work for me or for Tucker. I will not put him through another Monday morning panic attack." I took out my phone, opened the "notes" section, and read all the symptoms and their severity to Dr. Will. I asked him to enter those on Tucker's chart and notify the psychiatrist so he could read them and give a prescription. I added that I was not going to leave the hospital without it. My plan worked. Tucker was prescribed Ativan for me to give him the next admission day.

Next, I worked with Tucker's social worker to get him into counseling—not just the regular counselor that I had Kayci and Siera going to every Monday, but one who specialized in what Tucker was going through. Fortunately, there were counselors at the U of M, and I was able to get him an appointment. Unfortunately, the only opening was on Thursday, not the following week when Tucker would be in the hospital anyway. When I took him out of class for this appointment, Tucker yelled and resisted in front of peers for the first time. Once I got him out of the classroom, he repeatedly put his foot down to stop his wheelchair. I was sweating as I struggled to get him into my van. He screamed the entire drive there, and of course there was traffic, making the hell last even longer. I wanted to cry and yell and quit this whole effort, but somehow I summoned the strength to stay calm. I repeated to myself, *This is why you are bringing him*; *this is just showing you he needs it.*

Thankfully, the appointment was just for Tucker, so once I got him settled in the counselor's office, I ran outside to the nearest bench and sobbed. It was one of the worst of the many, many bad hours that had transpired since this nightmare began, what felt like an eternity ago.

After this appointment, Tucker's second week "off" went much better. It ended with all three kids having a good weekend with their dad and all their friends in St. Michael; Kevin and I took advantage of the free time and went to Red Wing, the place of our first road trip a couple years earlier. At long last, Kevin did propose, and I was thrilled to say yes. It was a nice escape from reality to just be out of town with him. But of course, with cancer, escapes are few and fleeting. As we drove home on Sunday, I was already worrying about how admission would go on Monday.

On Monday morning I tried to give Tucker the Ativan, but he refused and started falling into a panic attack. Instead of hiding, Kayci was ready for what was going to happen and chose to come sit by Tucker on the couch as I packed. She held his hand, using her other hand to rub his back, and told him it would be OK and that he should take the medicine.

Once again, I kneeled down before Tucker with the medicine in my hand. As Kayci held his hand and told him to please take it, Tucker did. Kayci rarely told her big brother what to do; he was the leader and she was his favorite and loyal sidekick, so her asking meant everything to him. Then, with Kayci still holding his hand, he shared that he hated going to the hospital because he missed his sisters too much. Kayci was crying quietly as they hugged each other. Siera, who watches and listens to everything, came over from where she was dressing her doll. Tucker reached out to her, and the three had a group hug and cried together.

Just then, I had an idea. I asked Kayci and Siera to each pick out a stuffed animal for Tucker to bring to the hospital. Then I asked Tucker to pick out a small stuffed animal that each of his sisters could bring to school. All three of them could hold the stuffed animal whenever they were missing each other. It was heartwarming to see each of them be very deliberate in choosing which stuffed animal would be the best one for their brother/sister. Then they sat on the couch, told each other why they'd picked the one they did, and hugged as they handed them over. The girls were late to school, and Tucker and I would be late to the hospital, but none of that mattered.

Then Tucker asked—actually insisted—that he come with me to bring the girls to school. I warned him it would be hard to stay in the car and pull away from ISLA. He acknowledged that but said he wanted to be with his sisters for as long as he could.

That afternoon, I told Tucker how proud I was that he had taken the new medication, and it had helped us get through the morning. It was a wonderful change. The doctors noticed it too. At one point we were all laughing at Tucker as he danced to one of Judd's favorite songs. The joking even continued when it was time for Tucker to give a urine sample. Despite Judd being there, Tucker always chose to have me help him. I took it as a testament of how connected we were through this battle. This time Tucker made an "accidental" wiggle while filling the cup. I know my son and his love of pranks, so I told him there was no way that was an accident as I put the cover on and washed urine off my hands. Tucker cracked up, and I laughed too. For every sample after, however, I was sure to put gloves on first, which would make Tucker laugh all over again. With cancer, you take the laughter wherever it happens, even in the restroom.

This week went much better than the first time. Tucker worked hard during his PT appointments and was already starting to use crutches. Tuesday night, Charlie and Greyson came to visit. I'd always known they were good friends, but agreeing to eat "Bean Boozled," disgustingly flavored jelly beans, was going above and beyond. The laughter and memories will remain forever, and I am sure the gross flavor seemed like it would last forever too. Tucker had some tears and anxiety when the boys left, but with the Ativan I had the nurse give him before the boys got ready to leave, he was able to talk about his feelings with me and then regained control of his emotions in about five minutes. I was so proud of him. Later, he almost started crying again when the Wild let the game get tied with seven seconds to go . . . and then lost in overtime. No med can help that.

That Friday would be his last dose of supercharged T before

scans. I was scared, and for a change I shared that in my CaringBridge journal entry:

I know you are all praying for Tucker, and I deeply appreciate it. I am asking for a few extra prayers for the next ten to twelve days. After that time, Tucker will get repeat CT scans of his lungs. We NEED results that show all of his spots are shrinking, not just some of them like last time with Plan A. This protocol is the only other known option that kills osteosarcoma in the lungs. If this doesn't work, the doctors would have to start figuring out which less proven options to try. I am lying here watching the last bag of T drip into my son's body before scans happen. Then we just hope these ten doses are killing everything they are supposed to be killing. And that my son is on his way to being "cancer free."

I hope we only have parents and adults reading these journals, and screening them before sharing with their children/Tucker's friends. Tucker knows he has a few spots in his lungs; that was part of his devastation during our last admittance. But he doesn't know that Plan B really, really needs to work. Nor will he ever know this, because I will never let him lose the positive attitude that he WILL beat this. Because he will. But he is nine and scared enough, so I don't want him to have any more bad news than is already right in front of him. So please, screen this info and do not share it with any children.

Love, Dana

I was more terrified than anyone knew, even more than I knew.

Chapter Thirty-Three

My kids and I needed a good distraction, and we got exactly that on our spring break. We took a two-day trip to Rochester, Minnesota, with Sara, Mason, and Paige, and, of course, Grandma and Papa. Cancer denies kids many normal activities; when they can get one back, it is a victory. For Tucker, this was swimming in the hotel pool. See? Nothing major for a normal kid and definitely nothing new for Tucker. But this time, as I watched Tucker swim, my eyes filled with tears of joy.

My son returned to something he'd done before. Other than the bald head and the look of nervousness as he swam to the deep end and started tiring, Tucker looked like a regular kid. I took a video of him swimming, of his very proud, beautiful smile when he reached the wall. I was cheering him on like he'd just won a gold medal. When a kid is beaten down by the beast that is cancer, every accomplishment takes as much work as Olympians put forth.

The second video I took was even more rewarding. I filmed Tucker in the shallow end, playing with his sisters and cousins. In that moment, Tucker was a regular kid. He was standing, laughing, and jumping around in the water. No walker. No wheelchair. No pain. No worries. The pool was magic. It gave Tucker his old life back. In waist-deep water, my son looked whole. Nothing had to be adapted or modified to include him. Even now I can shut my eyes and remember this scene and how profound it was. Those moments when I could forget about cancer were treasured, because the "new normal" was so very different from what my son's and family's lives had been just five months ago.

Though I was nearly full of joy, soon reality hit and the fantasy was over. Tucker had to get out of the pool because he was exhausted and cold. No longer was he a regular kid, as none of the other kids had even started to tire; he sat alone on my lap, wrapped in a towel, while the other kids continued to swim, laugh, and play. *Damn you, cancer.*

I brought him to the whirlpool to warm up. There, his swim shirt clung to his chest, and his port was clearly visible, including the little scabs where the needles punctured his skin. *Not a regular kid. It isn't fair.* I wanted to cry, my heart breaking for my cold, sick, skinny boy. But that was the one thing I could not do. Instead, I called Papa and the other kids over to join us so we could go back to trying to pretend Tucker was a regular kid. The playing and laughing resumed; kids are magical that way. Parents are magical too. We can make our pain disappear, stuffing it deep inside, and pull out a beaming smile to reassure our children that everything is fine.

As I went to bed that night, I was excited that Tucker got to share a bed with Kayci, best friends snuggled in next to each other. I was also happy to have my littlest sleeping buddy next to me. (Throughout the night this would turn into "on me," "over me," and "kicking me." Yes, Siera is a gymnast even when she sleeps!)

Before falling asleep, I reflected on how badly I wanted Tucker to be a regular kid. It was time for me to accept that he wouldn't ever be "regular" again. Even with a prosthetic, his body would be different forever. Many activities would need to be modified, and adaptations would be necessary. Eventually I thought, *Dana, your son won't be regular, but he can be exceptional. That must be why this is happening to him. Accept the amputation, get the damn cancer out of his body, and watch him go be far beyond regular. Tucker is going to knock this out of the park, figuratively and literally. Remember, there is nothing you and Tucker can't do.* I was able to find joy with these thoughts, and with these children of mine by my side.

My little self-pep-talk set the stage for our group hike the following day. When my mom suggested the plan, I am sure she was thinking of the nicely paved trails through the state park around the quarries in Rochester. As a forty-six-year-old out with a group of three little kids, one medium kid, and one big kid with only one leg, I was thinking the same thing. But that's no fun. Sara and I started on a trail with Tucker in his wheelchair, but we came prepared with the walker in case he wanted to switch things up. I believe it is always good to have options.

The walk started with my usual approach of making adventures fun but also educational. Sara and I had the kids stop at each sign and read the information about the history of the quarries. I thought that, as Tucker was the best reader of the group, he would feel important sharing the facts with his little cousins and sisters, but it became apparent this was not nearly as rewarding or enjoyable for him as I hoped.

My kids and I had hiked here the year before with Jayden and his family, spending hours climbing, hiking, and exploring the huge hills and dense forests within the park. I could feel that Tucker was remembering the fun of last year and was upset with his new, limited body forcing us to stay on the paved pathways.

The girls probably were too, but they were doing a great job of not talking about it.

Tucker started getting crabby and asked to go back. He was refusing to use his walker and wouldn't read any more signs. I knew what we needed to do. Or I should say, where we needed to go. "Let's go see what's up there!" I exclaimed as I pointed at a skinny footpath up the big hill. "I think there is an old cave over there, isn't there, kids?" Sara looked at me, wondering what my plan was. "Tucker, get out of your chair and let's get up this hill and check it out."

Sara pointed out the little hiccup with my plan: "What do we do with his wheelchair?" she asked me.

After a pause, I finally responded, "I'll just carry it." (*Good one, Dana—it's so light, streamlined, and easy to carry.*) "Come on, everyone! There's nothing we can't do!" I shouted, and we headed up the hill.

Kayci went first, with Tucker right behind her, advising her on how to maneuver around, over, and under the trees and rocks. I was carrying the wheelchair right behind Tucker. I think my plan was to drop the wheelchair and catch him if he were to fall backward—I didn't say it was a great plan, but it was a plan nonetheless. Sara was in charge of getting the three little ones up the hill without slipping in the mud or getting branches snapped across their faces. The path was definitely not designed for a walker, but we figured it out and got to the top! We all high-fived and cheered as we looked down the big green open area that was on the other side of the hill.

Another unexpected change of plans occurred when one of the kids wanted to roll down the huge hill. I wanted to say no—I knew Tucker couldn't as it would hurt his stump, maybe his port, and it just wasn't a good thing for a kid on chemo to do. But the other kids started running and rolling down the hill, so why not? I told Tucker to get in the chair and we would race them down the hill. Tucker gave me a questioning look, one I should have heeded. But I didn't—I was too caught up in our motto and told him to get in!

As I started jogging down the hill, Tucker started laughing. His laughter was like fuel, and I jogged a little faster. That was a mistake. The hill was so steep that I got too much momentum; soon I was running my fastest, terrified my son was going to go flying out of the wheelchair. I am sure Sara was too. I was honestly very scared, but Tucker's laughter was giving me the strength to move my old body faster than it had run since my college soccer days, twenty-four years earlier. I had visions of Tucker, me, and the wheelchair in a pile at the bottom of this hill.

Thankfully, that didn't happen. Not only did we arrive with Tucker still in his chair and me still upright, but we had beaten the rest of the kids! We'd had an advantage; they had to dive out of the way so I didn't run them down with the wheelchair, since I had absolutely no control to steer it. But nevertheless, we won! There were many high-fives and cheers, though not from me, as it took several minutes to catch my breath. It was so fun. Terrifying, but fun.

Now we were down the hill, but on the wrong side of where we needed to end up. We had to travel around the huge hills back through the woods and try to find a path out of there. I asked Sara if she would mind taking a shift pushing Tucker for a while, as I was still recovering. It all looked familiar, so I felt like we were doing well. Before long we would eventually get back to Grandma and Papa, who were waiting for us in the bird sanctuary by the parking lot. I had obviously forgotten what lay ahead, which was a big oversight on my part.

We now stood at the top of a narrow, very steep gorge about twenty feet long. If we could get down it, we would be on the path that led straight to the parking lot. If we couldn't, we would have to go back the way we came. Sara wanted to turn back; the reasonable part of me did too, but I knew the kids and I had made it down there last year, so I worried it would send a message to Tucker that we all couldn't do something because of him. I did not want to send that message. So once again: "Come on! There's nothing we can't do!" I yelled.

Now just to figure out how. I concluded I'd better go first and hike backward so I could be holding Tucker. But I had the walker and the wheelchair to deal with too. The wheelchair was no help, so I had Sara hand it to me, then turned around and sent it down the gorge on its own. I wasn't sure what I would tell Tucker's PT if I returned the thing in pieces, but I would worry about that later.

Next, the walker. He would need that once we got halfway down the gorge, so . . . *I know. I'll just hang it on a nearby branch and grab it after Tucker is in a stable place.*

Now Tucker had to lower himself down. I was holding him under the arms, but he was scared. This time, his fear fueled my strength. "I've got you. I promise." (Maybe that should have been my motto; it is definitely how I'd felt every single moment since that damn November 4 call.) Slowly, Tucker twisted his foot back and forth to inch down the steep ravine, using his arms to grab what he could to help steady himself.

It took a little while, but we did it! I even remembered to

grab the walker out of the tree so he could stand at the bottom and look up at his huge accomplishment while I walked back up and helped the rest of the kids down one by one. I think Tucker felt even more proud of himself when he saw that everyone else needed help too. Even Sara!

Finally, we were all down and on the tar path. I didn't mind one bit when Tucker said he wanted to finish the way in the wheelchair. I did too! But there was only room for one, so I walked, and the kids were excited to take turns pushing Tucker.

When we eventually got back to Grandma and Papa, they asked, "What took so long?" Telling them about our hike took almost as long as doing it. It was just a lot less exhausting.

Chapter Thirty-Four

The Rochester trip was a perfect start to the week, and ended up being Tucker's only forty-eight hours of a break from cancer stuff. We got back on Tuesday morning so he could get his blood draw. On Wednesday, he had to go to a counseling appointment down at the hospital, and there was another blood draw on Thursday. Each of these days Tucker cried that he "never gets a break" from this. I reminded him that he had Friday off, which wasn't much consolation. What's worse, it didn't happen.

Thursday's blood counts showed that Tucker's hemoglobin was too low, so he needed to go in for a blood transfusion . . . on Friday. I begged for him to be able to go on Thursday as he had plans with his friends on Friday, but they were too booked to squeeze him in. Poor Tucker not only lost his one no-appointment day, he had to be accessed and spend the day in the Journey Clinic. He stayed at Judd's house that night, so I lay awake in bed, worried about him and his anxiety. It turned out my worrying was warranted. Tucker threw up during the night and hardly slept.

Kevin and I drove out to Judd's house Friday morning so Judd and I could take Tucker to the Journey Clinic together. He hadn't brought Tucker in before, and it was definitely a two-person job. Tucker was miserable and needed to be carried to the car. Both his anxiety and his sadness were high, and there was no Ativan since it wasn't a planned admission. At the clinic, we were all happy when we were told he only needed one needle accessed. That joy was quickly dashed when his vitals were taken and his temperature was 99.7. *Please no. If it gets above 100.4 he needs to be admitted.*

The transfusion needed to be postponed to see what would happen with his temperature. The four-hour ordeal was getting longer, and Tucker's time with his friends and sisters was getting shorter. The day was going from bad to worse.

It hit rock bottom when Tucker did end up getting admitted. His fever hit 101, so now he did need to have both needles inserted and to be admitted to the hospital. Tucker had already been accessed with the one needle; now, only hours later, all that tape had to be ripped off his skin so that the second needle could be shoved into his chest and more tape put on. All this on the one day that was supposed to be just playing with friends. But cancer doesn't care about your plans or your friends. It doesn't care about you or your life. It wants to destroy both.

Tucker ended up also needing a chest X-ray and additional oral medications. Then I had to break it to him that he would have to stay overnight. It was horrible. So horrible. As a mother, you just have to ask yourself how much more your child can take. And how does he get through it, not just for the day, but for many more months?

We got up to the hospital room and finally started the blood transfusion around 5:00 p.m., seven hours after arriving. That was cut short when, at 6:30, Tucker's temp spiked to 102.5 degrees. They had to stop the transfusion just in case it was causing the fever, although it most likely wasn't. Ironically, we had come in for a transfusion and got everything but that.

What made things even more sad was that it was Kayci's

birthday. Luckily Jack's mom, Cheri, took care of the girls all day, and then brought them, her three kids, and Siera's best friend Brooke to the hospital to celebrate Kayci's birthday there. They had made Tucker and Kayci's favorite orange jello, and we used straws for candles. Another mom skill: making the best of a crappy situation. It was great to have a party for Kayci after all, and for Tucker to be surrounded by friends.

Unfortunately, it had to end. I ordered the Ativan and started the painful goodbye process. As Tucker yelled that he wanted to go too, he cried, "I'm like a baby bird stuck in a nest and can never leave." He kept crying, "I want to be free!"

Oh honey, I want nothing more than for you to be free. Free of needles and medicines, free of finger pokes and appointments, free of poisons that have now taken out your eyebrows and eyelashes as well. Free to stay home and play every minute that every other child gets to. I want you free of this horrible life with cancer.

It was also Easter weekend, so once again I had the fear of Tucker being in the hospital on a major holiday and missing another family get-together. I knew the A-Team would postpone things if that were to happen, but it still would be sad to be stuck in the "nest." Saturday, it wasn't looking good that Tucker would be discharged; the doctors told us to plan on spending Easter Sunday in the hospital. I asked if there were any possibility of getting out at any time on Sunday, begging the doctors once again and telling them how much Tucker needed the mental health boost of a family holiday at Grandma and Papa's house. They compromised with me and said they would take his labs at 1:00 p.m. on Sunday instead of 5:00 p.m. to see if he could get out midday.

The A-Team rallied around Tucker and relocated Saturday

night's Wild and Egg Dyeing party to Tucker's hospital room. All four of my siblings brought their families to spend the afternoon and evening with us. Judd and his girlfriend joined us too. The Wild won, and the cousins colored five dozen eggs. Everyone enjoyed creating and laughing together.

I was surprised when I found out that Kayci had assumed the Easter Bunny wouldn't come to the hospital and complained about being with her brother instead of getting an egg hunt and candy in the morning. *Silly girl, of course they will have an egg hunt to enjoy.* Kevin scurried around gathering and buying all the supplies during the day. Then, at 10:30 p.m., I snuck down to the parking garage to get the stuff, hoping this was the only time I would ever need to prepare baskets and fill plastic eggs in a hospital bathroom.

The next trick was worrying about how Tucker would "hunt" for eggs. I knew the girls would share with him and help him, but he already was so aware of what he couldn't do, so I didn't want him to experience that again. Luckily, the Easter Bunny hid one-third of the eggs really close to Tucker or on his wheelchair and walker. I was happy to find thirty-nine hiding spots in the hospital room. It wasn't what any of us wanted, but I hoped the kids would still have fun.

The kids were thrilled to discover the Easter Bunny does come to hospitals. Tucker was able to find lots of eggs, and they all loved the candy and presents in their baskets. It was so great to hear their giggles and laughter while they "hunted." I love holidays, and being a mom is the best part. You get to provide so much joy for your kids. I also love having traditions, and I am so glad we didn't have to break them, just modify them. I will always do that for you, my wonderful children.

Then we finally got some good news: Tucker, and the party, would be at Grandma's and Papa's as planned! I didn't even say "I told you so" to the doctor, instead giving him a hug and thanking him for agreeing to change the protocol of waiting until 5:00 p.m. to do the draw. We hurried and packed up everything, then went straight to Bloomington. When the kids walked in, there was more cheering than at a Wild game! Like Mason said, "The party is wherever Tucker is!"

Once you are a parent of a child with cancer, however, there is no party that can shut out the anxiety of impending scans and the terrifying follow-up meeting to hear the results from the doctors. While the cousins laughed and hunted for eggs, I was hiding my anxiety and nausea about tomorrow's scans. Tucker needed an Easter miracle.

Chapter Thirty-Five

Monday, scan day, was hard for all of us, but mostly for Tucker, of course. Judd and I watched as the nurse had to poke and re-poke Tucker's arm trying to get the vein to work. Then there was another insertion; blood squirted out, causing Tucker to scream. Next, poor Tucker still had to do a finger poke for more blood tests, then the CT scan and the bone scan. Finally, he was done.

I had Papa there with the hope that Tucker would go to the last hour of school. I was worried I might cry at the results meeting and that if Tucker saw me, he would think he was not going to survive. But Tucker refused to go to school without me. He insisted on sitting in the waiting room with Papa, so he was only one hundred feet down the hall from the meeting room. *That doesn't leave me much time to cry, recover, and get the redness out of my eyes. It had better be good news so my son will see happy faces on me, Judd, Kevin, and Lisa when we walk out.*

Tucker saw happy expressions, but there wasn't much truth behind the smiles. The scans showed "mixed results." Those were the words of the oncologist nurse practitioner, with Dr. Will by her side. Dr. Weigel was out of town at a conference. The one "medium"-size spot had been eleven millimeters and had now shrunk to five. However, there were four spots that had measured four millimeters which had all *grown* to five. Maybe one went to six—I was too busy trying not to burst into tears to remember.

They concluded that after looking at the results, there would not be a surgery to go in and remove all the spots in one of Tucker's lungs. Instead, they would try two more rounds of this supercharged T. Then we would repeat the scans to see if the spots were just being stubborn and needed more poison to blast at them before shriveling up and going the hell away.

I remember asking tons of questions, and not liking any of the answers:

"Why can't we do the surgery anyway?" Because it would be putting Tucker through a lot just to have new spots come back.

"If this doesn't work, are we stuck with just waiting for trials to hope he fits into?" Yes, we would look for other options. Maybe there was an ounce of positivity in her voice, but my brain didn't detect any.

"Should I start getting on websites and Google and find something to try?" We don't know about those websites, and Dr. Weigel knows what there is to know, so she will take care of it. Which sounded great, but then I thought, *She doesn't know what to do, because if she did, they would have told me there was a Plan C. So, there must be nothing left to try!* I internally screamed.

But I continued with one more question: "Has this protocol ever worked after four rounds even when it didn't after two?" The answer (this one is a direct quote, since I wasn't able to unhear this word for a long time): "Occasionally." I knew I was not supposed to ask percentages, but that sounded like a very, very small number.

With that, I was silenced. Not only was I consumed with

fear, I knew we had to get out of that room, as Tucker was counting every minute the four of us were in there.

It only took about ten seconds to walk from the room to Tucker and Papa, not at all enough time to recover from that news. As I predicted, Tucker immediately asked what the scans showed. I did not do as good of a job as I should have. I had to look up so my tears wouldn't trickle out of my eyes. Tucker repeated his question, this time asking if the black Legos were gone. My answer was, "Your small spot shrunk down to a tiny spot! But those few, silly tiny spots are still there. But remember, we knew 'mop-up' would be many months because black Legos need lots of T to kill them all the way." Tucker seemed quite satisfied with that answer. I wasn't in the least. But for the moment, I couldn't go there.

As I walked with Tucker back to the car, my mind spinning, somehow it spun to Kayci's birthday. With all the worry about Tucker's hospital stay and Easter, I had totally forgotten to do anything about Kayci's birthday when my whole family was together—she'd had her party at the hospital with her St. Michael friends, but no A-Team celebration yet. Now I was failing my healthy child too! How did I let this happen?

I called Sara's husband, Cap, in a total panic and asked if his sister still managed the Dave & Busters—if so, could she get us a table for tonight? Thirty minutes later, it was all arranged. I sent a group text out to the A-Team and Kevin's parents, who were in town from Florida. At six o'clock, Kayci arrived to her birthday party with twenty-five family members sitting around the table celebrating her. Everyone dropped their plans, got gifts, and sped over to the restaurant. There were balloons, a cake, and lots of tokens for all the cousins. The aunts and uncles played too. For a few hours, Kayci was surrounded by her favorite people and all the attention was on her, something that hardly ever happened for the healthy siblings.

I was still in shock over the scan results, and angry that I had forgotten to celebrate my daughter's birthday. But I was also amazed and grateful how, once again, the A-Team had saved the day and helped me take care of my children. I am so lucky to have been born into this family.

That night after the kids were finally asleep, the shock wore off. I kept hearing the word "occasionally" and couldn't fall asleep. For the first time ever, I "went there." I went to a dark, sad, terrifying place. I hadn't considered my worst fear since November 5, but now it was unleashed and emotions took over my brain.

For seven days, I couldn't stop thinking that Tucker was going to die. I didn't eat or sleep much at all. I could hardly smile, let alone laugh. Luckily Tucker was feeling good enough to sleep in the girls' bedroom with them so I could cry myself to sleep, or lie awake trying to shake the images of his funeral. I considered calling Dr. Weigel, hoping she would be able to say something to cast away my fears, but I couldn't bring myself to hear more bad news or even the same bad news. *What if?* I let horrible non-facts overwhelm me to the point that I lost hope for a little while. That made me so ashamed I hated myself and didn't tell anyone how negatively I was thinking.

I don't know why, but I eventually shared these thoughts with my coworker and friend Christa. I even admitted my feelings that Tucker might die, how I couldn't find my strength were that to happen. The next day, Christa came to work with her Team Tucker Go shirt on. She walked into my office and said, "It is OK that you have lost your hope for a little bit. It doesn't mean you are a bad mom. What it means is that now we, Team Tucker"—she pointed to her shirt—"step up and lead for a little while, while you recover. I know you will soon; and then you will take over the lead once again." This profound statement was the buoy that I clung to the week I was lost in a dark, cold ocean of despair and couldn't see land.

That Monday, admission day, I was a zombie as we went through the hell of bringing Tucker into the hospital. After his blood draw, Judd took Tucker out as I waited for the results. As I sat there by myself, I summoned up the strength to ask Dr. Weigel some questions. I was dreading hearing all the same information, but since she hadn't been at the last meeting, perhaps there was something that could be answered better, or maybe she would just be better at hiding the doom in her voice and body language.

Dr. Weigel's results review was so much better: "There was no evidence that this wasn't working." Right away I felt one hundred times better. She went on to say, "The fact that the one shrunk so much is good—do you realize how small one millimeter is?" Yes, I did, but I didn't know if it was still "small" in the world of tumors. She explained she would not have recommended two more rounds of this if there were any evidence that it wasn't working or wouldn't work. She was "hopeful." She couldn't guarantee it, but there was definitely reason to hope that this chemo would work.

With renewed hope and strength, I was able to ask if there were more things to try should this not work. Dr. Weigel said there were many. Dr. Will was there with us, and I told him, "You can hug me this time." He knew what I was referring to and chuckled as he gave me a hug. At the results meeting last week he'd started to hug me, but I'd adamantly refused because it would make me fall apart, and I couldn't let Tucker see me like that.

Then I hugged Dr. Weigel, which I don't think was typical, certainly not for me. But I had to thank her not only for being brilliant and dedicating her life to saving my son and all the other poor children stricken with this horrific disease, but for helping me out of my darkness and back into reality. Not a great reality, but one where my son had every possibility of eventually beating this disease.

Chapter Thirty-Six

I like to think I was making good decisions on how to take care of Tucker. One of my most regrettable choices, however, was the Thursday evening after the third round of supercharged T. The kids were at Judd's house, but when Judd determined Tucker's temperature was 100 degrees, he immediately brought them back to my house and then went home. I was both sad and frustrated that all this was my problem. Judd didn't understand how emotionally and physically hard it was to get Tucker into a car to transport him to the hospital. I was angry he hadn't just taken them all straight to the ER and had me meet them there. Perhaps it was out of this frustration that I didn't think through my plan.

I decided to let Tucker watch the Wild game while I put the girls to bed. I didn't want them to see the painfully sad process of extracting him from the house. Once they were asleep, I checked Tucker's temperature; it was 100.4 degrees. I let him watch the rest of the second period while bringing all our hospital gear through the back door and loading the car. In my efforts to spare Kayci and Siera from waking up to Tucker's screams, I didn't tell Tucker what his temp was. Instead I texted Kevin, who was sitting next to us, to walk to the door like he was leaving, but really hold it open, as I was going to pick up Tucker and carry him out to the car.

Without warning, I picked him up and walked out the

door. Tucker was shocked and asked where I was taking him. I told him, then dashed down the front steps as he screamed "NOOOOOOOO!" Dayra was there to shut the house door as Kevin opened the car door and I abducted my own child. *If only I could steal him away from this hell; instead I am taking him away from his exciting weekend plans, bringing him to the place he dreads.*

Tucker yelled at me relentlessly the whole way to the hospital. I restrained him again, holding him firmly as I repeated, "Yes, it isn't fair. You are right, it isn't fair." I couldn't let go to wipe his tears, so they dripped onto his Wild blanket while mine trickled down my face. Tucker later told me he hated how I did this. I promised I would never do it that way again. I am still mad at myself for having done this to my child.

Going to the emergency room was so emotionally traumatic. The surprise of it and how it ruined plans was devastating. Also, you had different doctors and nurses that needed lots of instruction, the beds were smaller, and the waits were bigger. It took until 1:30 a.m. to get Tucker up to the fifth floor. Finally, he could fall asleep and Lisa could go home. She was my partner in the ER; I could stay with Tucker while she made sure everyone knew and followed the Tucker-protocols. Her nephew would not be put through any additional emotional trauma.

Tucker didn't have a fever the following day, but they couldn't release him because his white blood cell counts were so low. The fever was from his own body's bacteria since there were no white blood cells to protect against it. We were told it could be a couple days for them to get to the normal range, and there was nothing we could do about it.

Tucker and I were both desperately hoping that his blood counts would jump so he could be released Saturday and go to

Jack's house for a Wild game party. Initially, it was looking good when his white blood cell count was in range, but our excitement was snuffed out when the nurse explained there was stuff inside the white blood cells, called ANC, that had to be at 500 before getting discharged. Tucker's was at 100. It did not look like he would make it to Jack's house. I was crushed, but not willing to let go.

My personality is not one to surrender. I have often been called stubborn, wanting things to go how I think would be best. I don't follow the established path if it doesn't lead to where I want to go. For example, during college I wanted to study abroad in Spain. St. Ben's, my college, had a program in Madrid, but I didn't want to stay there. I had a family in northern Spain that I had known and loved since meeting them during high school, so I wanted to stay with them. Choosing which thing I want is another thing I'm not accustomed to. I wanted both things: to stay with my Spanish family AND get college credits for attending classes. I never saw these traits as a flaw because I was willing to work as hard as necessary to get my desired outcome. To make this work, I looked through books about Spain, wrote letters to my Spanish family, and then made many expensive phone calls, from landlines, between two and six in the morning, calling university admission offices in Asturias, Spain. I figured out how to find and enroll in courses and then worked with professors at St. Ben's to get them to approve my courseload. My work paid off. I earned sixteen credits while living with my amazing and loving Spanish family in Gijon and attending La Universidad de Oviedo.

I believe that being stubborn for a good reason is an asset, and should be called determination. I don't believe I "manipulate people" as much as I explain to them the benefits of my proposals, which are highly thought out with all factors considered. Maybe stubbornness could be a bad trait if used with bad intentions. But I always have good intentions. During my adulthood, they were to help fix the damaged lives of children. And at this moment, my intention was to protect my son's mental health and get him to his buddy's house so he could laugh and play with his friends.

The doctor said Tucker would have another blood draw at six o'clock. I asked why at that time, and they explained it was a shift start time. I begged them to please redo his labs that afternoon at four o'clock, which would give him enough time to get discharged, de-accessed, and to St. Michael before the Wild game started. The doctor said he had never had that request before, but my "stubbornness" paid off: the doctors agreed to an earlier blood draw, and I was grateful.

Before they left, one doctor told me how to "cheat." I was all ears. He explained that exercise makes the white blood cells come out of the bone marrow. *Why is he just telling me this now? Yesterday Tucker was so depressed that I just let him lie in bed all day.* The doctor recommended that at 3:30 I have Tucker do some exercise to give him a better chance at higher counts.

I was going to do better than that. I went back into the room and told Tucker the news. He started yelling and bawling, but I stopped him and said we didn't have time for that. I got him into his pajama pants, his sock, and his shoe while he continued to cry. Then I put his walker in front of him and pushed him out the door—not literally, of course. I told him I needed a Diet Coke and he needed a workout. I had him walk all the way to the cafeteria and back.

Back in the room, he needed another red blood transfusion, so I put in the movie with the perfect theme for our plan: *E.T.*, a little guy who also wanted to go home. Tucker and I cried for poor Elliot. When it ended, I told Tucker to get up and do the warm-ups I saw him do in phys ed class. He did jumping jacks, took a lap around the floor, and shot some hockey pucks and nerf hoops to stay active.

At 3:55, I took Tucker out for one more lap around Floor Five. A little before 4:00, the blood-draw guy arrived. Kevin came out into the halls to find us. I told him to go to the room and stall, saying that he saw us but it would take a couple minutes for Tucker to walk back to the room. I wanted to make sure Tucker finished the lap. When we arrived back at the room, I felt like my child should do the same dance Rocky did when he reached the top of the steps in Philadelphia.

While we waited for the lab results, I was making Tucker aware that the A-Team was on standby to come watch the game with him if he didn't get out tonight, and that Cheri and I had arranged another party at Jack's Monday night. If we did need the backup plan, I hoped there was enough Ativan for both of us. Judd came down to the hospital hoping to bring Tucker home, but ready to stay and watch the Wild game down there with the A-Team if needed.

At five o'clock, the doctor arrived. Everyone was quiet as I asked her for the number. She replied, "Five hundred." I told her we all knew that was the number we needed to reach; what was Tucker's number? She repeated, "Five hundred. Exactly. Tucker's ANC count is five hundred."

Cheers of joy could be heard all the way out into the hall. Thank goodness we hadn't cut that last lap short!

We moved like a well-trained MASH unit tearing down camp as Tucker slammed some meds. Kevin packed up my stuff and Judd packed up Tucker's. Tucker did his fastest de-accessing ever and was in Judd's truck by 6:10. I called Jack to tell him the great news, and once again cheers erupted. An hour later, I got a call that Tucker was in Jack's living room a minute before the puck dropped. A win for the good guy!

Chapter Thirty-Seven

The next round of supercharged T was another social week for Tucker in the hospital. On Tuesday, Kylie Bearse, of WCCO's morning news show, came to meet and interview him. He was ready for her, wearing an orange hoodie, orange shorts, and an orange sock. We also got his hockey net set up so he could show her, and all the viewers, how he had taught himself to shoot wrist shots while balancing on his one leg. Of course, Tucker wanted to hide his IV pole and sit on the couch for the interview. He never wanted pity, even though it was well deserved. Tucker wanted to show people what he could still do and hoped they didn't notice what he couldn't do.

Like the others, Kylie was smitten with Tucker, so impressed with his knowledge of the Wild as well as his physical accomplishments. He made her laugh out loud when he talked about some of the advice he had given Jason Zucker about his game. Only my son would let everyone know he called Jason a "puck hog" and told him he needed to "shoot more." Jason told me that his Wild coach has said the same thing. Maybe Tucker would be the first coach in the NHL who didn't play professional hockey.

Judd had come to the hospital to be there for the interview. Since he was there, I left to have lunch with Mom and Kevin. We were talking wedding plans. Originally, I'd wanted to wait until Tucker was better and cancer was behind us. I didn't want the wedding photos to have skinny, bald Tucker, causing us to always think of cancer when we looked at them. However, Kevin and my mom thought it would be something fun to work on and look forward to during these dark times.

While looking at the calendar on my phone, I noticed that June 11 fell on a Saturday. That was my grandparents' wedding date, and my grandpa had died two months before they could celebrate their fiftieth anniversary. I took that as a sign that I shouldn't wait. Kevin and I agreed that we would get married on June 11 in my parents' beautiful backyard, full of flower gardens and family memories. My sisters and brothers were excited about the news, and all were helpful in the planning and execution of another A-Team wedding.

When I returned to the room, Kevin and I shared the news with Tucker. After all, he was the best man. Kevin had asked him the week after we were engaged; I don't think there was a man more deserving of the title. Kayci and Siera were going to be my junior bridesmaids.

In hindsight, I see now making such a monumental decision during a time of intense stress and fear of loss was not wise. That would become very clear to both Kevin and me over the coming months and years. However, at the time, when drowning in so much fear and pain, it was my instinct to grab the life preserver of happiness Kevin provided.

We had another fun event to enjoy on Thursday at the hospital: Masonic had its annual superheroes party to celebrate all the brave patients, who truly are heroic. All the doctors and nurses dressed in superhero costumes. Sara brought Mason and Paige to the party, and Judd brought Kayci and Siera. We got them out of school so they could celebrate their big brother.

Cousin Sophie even came up from Gustavus College. We all headed down to the lobby, where the kids made wristbands, got their faces painted, played games, and enjoyed the loud music while mingling with all sorts of superheroes in full costumes. It was a very fun afternoon.

The day got even better when Jason and Carly came to visit Tucker. While Carly and I talked mutual wedding plans, Sara and Sophie brought all the kids to a movie down in the hospital's auditorium so Tucker could have some time to just hang out with Jason. In addition to their usual hockey talk, Tucker loved learning all about Jason's childhood hockey days and teams. Of course they played Xbox hockey a bunch, enough that Jason even got his first win against Tucker. I loved watching Tucker be so happy; I still couldn't believe his sports hero liked Tucker as much as Tucker liked him.

After Jason and Carly left, Kayci and Siera also said goodbye. It would be too much for everyone to leave at once, so Sara stayed for a little while longer. With her, Mason, and Paige in the room, I was able to leave and walk the girls out to the car. Their lives had been turned upside-down just like Tucker's, but they didn't have the consistency of their mom by their side. Siera especially was having a hard week—so many tears Sunday night, Monday night on the phone, and when I saw her at Grandma-care Tuesday night for dinner. Kayci was trying to be extra strong for her sister, but no one could get Siera to stop crying at these times of separation. My baby girl was only five years old. Typically, kindergarten is the biggest challenge at that age, but Siera was enduring so much more.

After saying goodbye to the girls in the parking ramp, I

went to a restroom in the lobby to cry. When I returned to Tucker's room, Mason yelled, "Dana, guess what!"

It was great to be greeted with excitement. "What, Mason?"

"I beat Tucker! I beat Tucker at Xbox!" Mason couldn't even sit. He was jumping with his arms in the air.

"Seriously? Wow!"

I looked over at Tucker, who nodded his head and said, "Yeah, he crushed me." I was very confused, even more so when Mason yelled out the score: "It was six to nothing!" he exclaimed, so incredibly proud of himself.

Tucker added, "I better practice some more before you come visit me next time." It was so sweet. Mason's smile couldn't get any wider. I couldn't get any more confused. Mason didn't even know how to play the game, hardly.

As Sara was getting the kids ready to go, she leaned over to me and told me that Tucker had pulled his goalie . . . for the entire game. He'd never let Mason catch on.

Oh my gosh, Tucker is the sweetest boy ever.

Chapter Thirty-Eight

While readying ourselves for the week of blood counts "bottoming out," we hoped to enjoy baseball and school beforehand. Monday, I drove the three kids up to St. Michael to watch the special baseball game between St. Michael-Albertville and Hopkins in Tucker's honor. Coach Schumm, Judd's friend and coworker, organized this "Strike Out Cancer" game. It was a wonderful and generous event from both communities. We enjoyed watching a great game, and Tucker cheered for both teams.

Right after, we had to hurry back down to Hopkins to get to opening night for Tucker's team. The thirty-five-minute drive turned out to be a cathartic time. Tucker cried the entire time, feeling bad that he made "everyone change their life." This was prompted by Judd telling Kayci he would not be able to chaperone her field trip that week, since he preferred to go to Tucker's appointment the same day. When Judd said this, Tucker was the first to cry. Such a sweet big brother, once again feeling bad for others as he sat in a wheelchair with one leg and suffering from chemo. Kayci started crying too; it was heartbreaking because I knew she didn't want to make Tucker feel bad. She was just so sad she couldn't stop herself.

As Tucker continued sobbing, he then started talking about how much he wanted to play baseball. He loved playing hockey; however, his connection to baseball was innate and his skills were remarkable. This season, instead of being the most valuable player, he would just be the assistant coach in the dugout. Tears were streaming down his face, and now Siera and I were crying too. I watched in the rearview mirror, helpless, wishing I could hold all three of my kids. What I saw next made me cry even more: Kayci found the strength to stop crying and leaned over so Tucker could put his head on her shoulder as she rubbed his back. My amazing kids.

I desperately wanted to keep driving, to think about anything other than the fact that my son, who lived for playing sports, once again had to sit on the sidelines and watch his buddies go do what he so badly wished he could do. My favorite thing to watch was Tucker at bat. He was a first pitch hitter, and every hit went right up the middle. He had a great stance—elbow up, weight on his back leg, hands chocked up just a little—and then as he settled in for the pitch, he would wiggle his butt side to side. Tucker loved batting, and his butt wiggle was like his own little happy dance that he was about to hit a line drive double. I selfishly wanted to skip the whole night because I couldn't bear to see him in a wheelchair instead of at bat.

I suggested to Tucker that we skip his team's game. "Everyone will understand if you don't go, Tucker," I told him, even though he was scheduled to throw out the first pitch. As we got closer to Maetzold Park, I asked again if we should just go home and rest.

Tucker didn't answer. As the field lights a block away came into view, he dried his eyes and said, "Mom, go to the field. They are my team." Once again, my son was stronger than anyone I know.

The girls and I brought Tucker to the field, where Coach

Bob wheeled him out to the mound so he could throw out the first pitch of the Hopkins Little League season. The teammates were lined up between Tucker and home plate, with Greyson behind the plate to catch it. Tucker took the ball and hurled a perfect strike. As the boys ran over to mob Tucker on the mound, there was a voice yelling, "WAIT! You have to do it again!"

The voice was mine. In my excitement, I hadn't hit record on my phone, and I definitely wanted this recorded. Tucker knew I was serious, but the others didn't, so I yelled again. "Seriously, we have to do the 'first pitch' again. Everyone back to your places!" Tucker laughed. He and his sisters went through this nearly every year on their birthdays when I didn't hit the right button to record a video and we had to re-light the candles to have them blow them out again.

I was nervous that Tucker couldn't do this twice in a row, but I should have never doubted the baseball boy. Another strike, and with oompf. The teammates mobbed Tucker again, then yelled to Bob, "Can we have Tucker pitch? He's better than the rest of us!" It was the first season of kid-pitch, so that statement was pretty accurate. Tucker was proud of himself not just for pitching the strikes, but for still being a ball player. I was so proud to even know Tucker, let alone get to be his mother.

Sunday was Mother's Day. Once again, Tucker rose to the occasion of being the oldest child and orchestrated breakfast in bed for me. I heard him say, "Girls, time to get up and make Mom breakfast." The next thing I heard was even better. Actually, it was what I didn't hear. I did not hear Tucker's walker or crutches. I peeked out my door and saw him hopping around the kitchen! Yes, he held onto furniture at times, but he could get around without crutches or a walker. When they were nearly finished making my breakfast, I stopped watching this beautiful sight and hurried back into bed.

Tucker made his delicious scrambled eggs, Kayci toasted the frozen waffles, and Siera had the very important job of pouring me a glass of Diet Mountain Dew on ice. Then they all gave me gifts that their teachers helped them make. Tucker made me a card at school. Señora Shrestha told me he asked if he could; it was not a class-wide project. He was a wonderful son. In his best handwriting, he wrote me this poem:

Mi Mama,
Los ojos de me Mama son el color del oceana,
y siempre es maravillosa.
Estas siempre conmigo.
Gracias, mamacita, por ser me madresita.
de Tucker

He decorated it and put it in an orange frame. I cherish it. Kayci made me a card that said I was her "Herow," which means so much to me because I always worried that my healthy kids resented me for spending so much time away. Siera made me a picture with tissue paper flowers, with "MAMA" in big painted letters, that is still hanging on my wall. The breakfast was wonderful. Having all three kids in my bed with me was even more wonderful.

Chapter Thirty-Nine

All night I fought hard to not think, *What if this is the last Mother's Day with all of us here?* This feeling was always looming, hoping to grab hold of my consciousness. I worked hard to fend it off, but the emphasis of it being Mother's Day coupled with the fact that Tucker's scans were the following day made it impossible to not go there. I knew Tucker was worried about his scans too. So, that night after I put the girls to sleep, Tucker and I cuddled up, and I told him all about our first Mother's Day together so we could focus on much more pleasant thoughts.

I am glad I was able to have some joy on Sunday, because there was not one iota of joy on scan day. This time just Lisa and I met with Dr. Weigel. I wanted Judd to stay with Tucker instead of Papa for two reasons: I think it was better for Tucker's distraction, and Judd has a harder time hiding his emotions. If it was bad news, I knew it would be really bad in the big picture of things, and Judd and I knew he wouldn't be able to keep it together.

This time even Dr. Weigel couldn't find a positive spin to the results. Every spot had grown. All of them. I didn't want many details after that; I had to keep my composure. That's why Lisa came, to track the details and hold my hand. Dr. Weigel explained we still had some options, but the chances of beating this were getting smaller and smaller. She went on to provide a wretched time frame, words no mother or father should ever have to hear.

After hearing "one to three years," I tuned out everything else that was said. Lisa didn't know this and wouldn't realize it until later. I didn't share those words or numbers with anyone, and I worked hard to "unhear" them. Truth be told, it worked. Because I did forget about those details, and I continued to fully believe my son was going to beat this. When Dr. Weigel finished talking, I asked, "So what's next?"

The best option would be a thoracotomy, which was a surgery to get the lesions out of Tucker's lungs. However, that could only happen if the surgeon thought he could get to all the spots. Dr. Weigel was still waiting to hear the verdict. She went on talking about other medicines with long names, but I was too busy trying not to stand up and punch the wall to even hear her. Instead, I held Dr. Will's hand—well, more like squeezed it in anger—and said, "This is just wrong." He agreed.

No time for tears—Tucker was waiting for me, and we had a Twins game to get to. I told the group we were going to say, "It turns out now we have two options [like it was getting better]: surgery or a different T. The doctors still have to talk about it to see which one is going to work better to get rid of the black Legos." There were not going be any "ifs" or "maybes." The team nodded; I reminded them that everyone needed to be smiling and upbeat.

I went to go get Tucker, a big smile on my face. This time, I brought him into the meeting room so he could see that Dr. Will and Dr. Weigel agreed with my version of the results. I didn't want him wondering if his mom was just giving him fake good news, which I was.

Tucker and Judd took the news well and asked about the surgery. I explained that the surgeon would make a cut into his side and then get out the few black Legos that were in his lungs. I told him they were so tiny the surgeon couldn't use a tool to find them; he had to use his fingers so he could find the little bumps.

Wow, my mom-reports were *so* much better than Dr. Weigel's. Her description of the surgery showed me how long the incision would be, from the front of his side all the way to the back of his side, large enough for the surgeon to get his entire hand inside my son so he could palpate the entire lung. I didn't like her version, but I did hope it would happen. After Tucker's one question, I said we needed to get going to pick up his sisters and get to Target Field to watch some Twins baseball. I even cheered as I stood up and took hold of his wheelchair handles. The power of denial was seemingly inexhaustible.

I drove Tucker home, shifting my head to make sure he couldn't see me in the rearview mirror. Tears kept welling up. We hurried Kayci, Siera, and Kevin into the car and were off to Target Field. We got a wonderful tour, and Tucker even got to meet Dick Breamear, the Twins announcer, and sit in his studio booth. The game started, but then rain set in and canceled it. Truthfully, I was relieved—I could not sit there and keep it together much longer.

Everyone else was asleep by 9:45, and I lay next to my boy in his bed. I can't put into words the fears that were consuming me. Dr. Weigel's numbers were haunting me. I made my mind up that Tucker needed that surgery; if the surgeon said no, I would talk him into it. He would have to listen to a pleading mother, right? I convinced myself I would make it happen and got a little bit of sleep.

Tuesday, I went to work but didn't really accomplish much as I was waiting for a call to hear yes or no on the thoracotomy. Finally, my phone rang at 12:30 and I got the news I wanted. The surgeon did think he could get to every spot and remove them, so he was approving surgery.

Falling to the floor, I sobbed like I had just won the lottery. I knew Dr. Weigel's numbers and words were wrong! I knew my son was going to make it! This was the first ounce of relief I'd had these whole damn six months. Yes, Tucker was going to beat this! I knew it! It was so confusing to feel happy after feeling completely devastated for the past twenty-four hours. Then I wondered if I was happier than I should be. I guess that is a trait of a cancer mom, always waiting for bad news and too afraid that good news is temporary.

We met with Dr. Acton, the surgeon, two days later. He gave us so many details, many I didn't want to hear. Tucker, Judd, Lisa, and I learned Tucker's situation, and it was much worse than I'd been aware of. Apparently my mom-reports were contorting my reality. Dr. Acton showed us Tucker's CT scans by traveling "down" through the "slices" of his lungs to point out how many tumors there were. I was very nervous about Tucker seeing this because I had always told him he only had five. I thought the real number was eight.

It wasn't. Dr. Acton counted one by one for what felt like seven minutes when he finally stopped at twenty-freaking-one. What the hell? And that was only Tucker's right lung. I think Tucker tuned out during the counting; I know I chatted with him hoping to distract him. The good news was that all the spots were on the periphery and easy to reach.

Thursday night, Tucker got through the pre-op shower with the horrendous-smelling antiseptic soap. He and I stayed up late cuddling on the couch and watching some of our TV shows. Friday morning did not go well at all, even with the Ativan. Tucker was miserable, starving, angry, and upset. He had an intense panic attack throughout the second sterile shower, screaming the whole time even as I dressed him. My ears were ringing, but I said nothing. Kevin carried him to the car, both of us hoping the screaming would stop. Not just for our ears, but for my shattered heart.

On the highway, we found out Tucker's door didn't have the kid-proof lock on, and I leapt to grab the handle and shut the door. Tucker wasn't only terrified of the surgery; he was devastated that he was missing fishing opener and time at the cabin. He didn't know that I could have chosen to wait until Monday, but even I couldn't put his mental health over his physical health when things were this dire. Finally, he stopped crying when we pulled up to the hospital. He let me lift him out of the car and into his chair. I hugged him—no words, just a long hug—then wheeled him into his prison.

Tucker's surgery went very well. The surgeon told us he was able to get all the black Legos. The best news was there were no new or unexpected tumors. Possibly even better news was that all but one spot was white and calcified, indicating that they could be dead. One was purple, meaning it was alive. I was so hoping it was the only one.

Papa had left to go get the girls from ISLA so they could come see their brother. Right when I started getting used to the sight of my kid hooked up to medicines, wires, tubes, and machines, in walked my eight-year-old daughter to see it. Kayci was terrified to see everything attached to Tucker in post-op. She asked if it was OK to touch him, then carefully rubbed her brother's bald but adorable head. I saw Tucker's mouth curve into a tiny smile while Kayci talked to him, so I told her that Tucker heard her and knew his best friend was there taking care of him.

So many kids to worry about. One child in post-op after having twenty-one pieces of his lungs taken out, another child with tears rolling down her cheeks trying to reassure her big brother he was fine, and then a third child crying by the elevators refusing to let go of me was just way too much for a heart to handle. I don't know how mine kept beating when it was in so many tiny pieces.

It was a harder recovery than I had anticipated. It took three days until Tucker started to feel better. Mom and Lisa came to visit and give me a break from Tucker's room since Judd was there that day. While eating in the cafeteria, Mom asked what the next steps would be now that the thoracotomy was done. I was tired of talking about it, and since Lisa knew all the details, I let her answer. Then Mom asked what the chances were for beating this. I jumped into the conversation and said, "Not great, only like 10 percent I think, but Dr. Weigel didn't say."

Then Lisa, who thought she was jogging my memory, said Dr. Weigel said that it would be "a long shot." I replied, "Yes, so like 10 percent, but now with the thoracotomy it will be even higher." Lisa didn't realize I had snapped from reality during that scan results meeting, so she explained how it would take a "miracle" for Tucker to beat this.

I looked at my sister with disgust. "How could you say your nephew isn't going to make it?" I yelled, not realizing or caring people around us could hear me. "You are supposed to be on our side!" Sobs burst out of me as I ran out of the building to the very edge of the hospital property. I found a bench and cried, hard. I was furious at Lisa for saying what she said.

I don't even know what I meant when I said that. To this day I can't believe I yelled at Lisa and accused her of not being on our side. All I know is that for months I was determined to beat this, but that day of the scan results I was told to just be "hopeful." I couldn't make that mental shift. I couldn't acknowledge "one to three years." Instead, I clung to my own reality. A reality that crashed down around me from the word "miracle," spoken by the person who was going to help me cross the finish line. As I sat in the shattered remnants of my false reality, the true one seeped in. I sobbed so hard I ended up in the fetal position on a cement bench.

I tried to accept that my son would not make it to his sixth-grade graduation. I tried to be like Lisa, aware of reality but still strong. But I couldn't. I reconstructed my false reality and had new resolve that my son was going to beat this. I got over my anger toward Lisa by telling myself that she had a more jaded outlook because of her twenty-five years working in a hospital. I told myself that it wasn't going to take a miracle—it would just take more work, but that was fine, I was ready for it and I would make sure Tucker was too.

I found Lisa and Mom and said, "I am sorry for yelling at you. You are emotional and scared too, so you just misspoke. I get it." Lisa knew she hadn't misspoken; she knew she had the facts right and I didn't. But instead of correcting me, she hugged me.

Chapter Forty

On Tuesday, Tucker once again shocked the doctors with how well he had recovered. While he was discharged, he and I stayed home from school on Wednesday to make sure he was resting and healing well. Truth be told, we had to keep up his strength so we could spend the evening at the ballpark. Tucker's team was eagerly awaiting his return to the bench. They missed him and his rule: when a kid struck out, before his next at-bat he had to rub Tucker's bald head for good luck. I laughed when Tucker told me about this, but he was serious. "Mom, watch, they don't get another strike-out. It helps them laugh, and everyone bats better when they're relaxed." Nine years old and already a coaching genius.

Tucker returned to school only six days after having a man's hand digging around inside him and taking out nearly two dozen pieces of his lung. He still had nerve catheters for pain meds and twenty-five stitches across his ribs. Nevertheless, he was refereeing the soccer game at recess. After school on Friday, Judd took him and the girls up to Grandpa's cabin for a very well-deserved weekend at the lake, fishing, enjoying the loons, and going on pontoon rides.

Tucker's job that weekend was to forget about the black Legos. I told him I would do the same, but that was a lie. My weekend was doomed after the call I received from the doctors on Friday. I was very grateful for my ability to hide my emotions so I could send the three kids off in Judd's car with a big smile on my face. Behind that smile were only pain and fear.

All twenty-one spots were "viable," or alive. It didn't sink in so much as it knocked me over. *So, the chemo that's like an atomic bomb did nothing, or at most just slowed down the damn cancer. Damnit!* Not one was dead. So no, I would not be forgetting about black Legos. Instead, I would be holding in this pain. I didn't want anyone else to be as low as I was. I was so sick of bringing everyone bad news and seeing everyone be sad. I have always been highly empathic and carry the weight of other people's pain, thus my need to fix things. Now, not only couldn't I fix it, but I was causing people pain whenever I shared it. I couldn't take much more.

Four nights later, I was getting Tucker ready for his second thoracotomy in eleven days. I was so proud of him for being physically and mentally strong enough to get through these two major surgeries in less than two weeks. Kayci and Siera were sad because once again their brother would be coming out in pain and covered in tubes and stitches. Tucker was brave, but he hated the pain of recovery and knew how bad it would be this time. It seemed like life couldn't get any worse.

Tucker and I were packed, along with the school lunches and gymnastics and baseball stuff for Kayci and Siera. I did find some relief in the fact that this would be my last time preparing for a hospital stay during the school year. The thought of no longer having to prepare notes and lesson plans for a substitute while also getting the girls ready with their stuff helped me power through that long, emotional, and anxiety-filled night.

However, as I finally laid my head on my pillow a few hours before the alarm went off, the rest of the doctors' report consumed my thoughts. This surgery was going to be more difficult than they had originally thought. The spots had been growing over the past two weeks without chemo, so Dr. Acton would have to take out more lung tissue than planned and was not sure if he would be able to remove a central spot safely. *This damn beast is working so hard to take my son away from me! Why? Why is there such an evil drive in those cells to devour healthy children and kill them? Why can't it be stopped? Why does it exist in the first place?*

After a couple hours of sleep, I went through the horrible routine of taking my boy from his comfy bed to the place he hated, into a room where everyone smiled and distracted, then onto the table where his little chest was sliced open so a surgeon could try to rid him of cancer. However, to Tucker and the public, I smiled, laughed, and expressed how awesome it was going to be to get all the black Legos out. It was harder to still get laughs the fourth time, putting on the space suit so I could hold my boy's hand all the way into the operating room and kiss his forehead until the medicine put him to sleep. As the sedating medicine started, I leaned down, stared into my son's gorgeous blue eyes, and told him that he was my hero. He answered, "I know, Mom. I love you."

I took my position in the waiting room, again flanked by my sisters, Mom, and Kevin. What a relief when it was over and we were informed that it "went well." They'd taken out twelve wedges from Tucker's left lung, and Dr. Acton believed he'd gotten clear margins on all of them. He warned us that recovery was going to be harder on Tucker this time since his right lung wasn't fully healed yet. He added that he was amazed how strong Tucker was to be able to get these surgeries so close together. I tried to focus on the positives, but I kept thinking about all the negatives. I just wanted to go hug my son.

When I got to Tucker's post-op room, I sat down, held his hand, and just cried. It was so wonderful to see him, and right now he had no cancer in him. He was still completely out, so I could just cry tears of joy that he was done with these surgeries. Tears of gratitude for Dr. Acton, who gave us the gift of time so we could find the correct chemo. Tears of fear that the cancer might already be trying to come back. Tears of exhaustion that this had been the hardest seven months of my life. Tears of suffering watching my son go through so much physical and mental pain. And tears of love, because I had so much for this little hero that I couldn't contain it.

That release proved to be exactly the catharsis I needed. By the time we got Tucker into his room, I was back. I put up those decorations, got some movies from the library in the lobby, filled the fridge with Diet Dew, and got myself a tasty Diet Coke from the cafeteria. When Tucker woke up, he was going to have the happiest and most positive mom on Floor Five. Dr. Acton had been successful, the tumors were out of my son's body, and the next treatment would be the one that destroyed this osteosarcoma once and for all. *Then I will just sit back and watch my son astonish everyone as he runs, hits, and fields better than ever with his prosthetic leg. It's going to happen. I know it. There is nothing we can't do!*

It was a good thing I restored my strength, because all my kids needed a lot of time and attention the following week. First, it was a grueling week of physical recovery for Tucker. He was confined to his wheelchair, couch, or bed for ten days. He couldn't use his crutches because of the stitches and tenderness under both arms along the side of his upper ribs. He couldn't use the walker because that required him to hop and the impact of landing was too painful on his lungs and ribs. To make matters worse, so much time in his wheelchair caused Tucker significant back and butt pain. The poor boy should have been running the bases and getting bruises from a bad hop of a grounder, not bruises on his butt from a wheelchair. I carried Tucker's oxycodone with me everywhere and set a timer so I was never a minute late for the next dose. I'm sure I had enough hours of massage experience on him to get licensed, as at least every hour I would try to relieve the pain from his little body. Señora Shrestha and his classmates did a great job of helping Tucker to the floor so he could do his work lying on his belly. At home, Kayci would do some massage too. It was a team effort to keep Tucker's pain at bay.

Nights were the hardest for Tucker. With both sides still full of stitches, he couldn't move without experiencing pain and waking up. He insisted on sleeping in his bed so he could be with his sisters, so throughout the night he would yell my name and I would hurry over and try to soothe his pain and anxiety. Now that he was immobile again, we were back to me helping him with his urinal bottles. Because his sides were so tender, I would kneel on the hardwood floor while massaging for thirty minutes at a time, trying to get him back to sleep. Every part of my body was sore too, but I knew my pain was just from age and the physical work required, not from something trying to destroy me or from a surgeon's hands in my ribs. Thus, it was easy to ignore any discomfort in my body. I just wished I could absorb all Tucker's pain.

Along with Tucker's recovery, all three kids were in their

last week of school. As every parent knows, that is a super busy time. Each kid had a concert to attend, projects to hand in, and library books to find. Siera had the extra fun event of kindergarten graduation. Of course my parents attended, and I got permission for Tucker and Kayci to come watch a little part of it. It was so wonderful for the whole family's attention to be on Siera for a change. There is never enough attention for the healthy siblings. Tucker was very aware of that too, so he did everything he could to make it to their baseball games and school events.

We made it through the crazy week. Tucker was sad to have school end; he loved being with those friends and his teachers. ISLA staff and students did such an amazing job of treating Tucker the same, but with a perfect blend of treating him special. Luckily, we still had baseball, another community that celebrated Tucker and fully supported Kayci, Siera, and me.

Chapter Forty-One

As the days passed, heading toward the next scan day on June 9, I worked hard to keep my fears and the possible reality of Lisa's "miracle" prognosis at bay. Apparently, I was successful in hiding my thoughts and tears—one night Tucker asked, "So Mom, I'm done with surgeries, right?" Before I could answer, he continued, "Oh, except for the one to remove my port when I'm all done with this."

I smiled and gave him a kiss on his forehead, reminding him yet again that he was my hero. I was so proud of Tucker for accepting this hell he had been unfairly given. And I must admit, I was proud of me for being able to hide my broken heart and the fear that took over my mind on a regular basis.

On June 8, while I was a nervous wreck about the next day's scans, I was happy that Tucker would have a wonderful distraction since his friend Owen had invited him over to play. They had a ton of fun, and I was hopeful that this would be the first of many playdates over the summer for Tucker. I used that time to have fun with Kayci and Siera, focusing only on them for a few hours. They loved every minute, and so did I.

That night, however, I did not love. There were only twelve hours left until Tucker got scanned. I wished it were a week ago so there was an even better chance of no new tumors. I was terrified but also wanted to get this over with, as the waiting had been hell. Not an hour had gone by where I hadn't said a quick prayer asking for there to please not be anything growing. At night I lay next to Tucker, putting my hand on his chest, and asked that it be quiet in there. It was unreal to not see or know what was happening, especially with so much hanging in the balance.

After scans came the dreaded results meeting with Dr. Weigel and Dr. Will. I was still traumatized from the last meeting with the latter and did not think I could face another one. It was like waiting for the movie star to open the envelope on Oscar night, but instead of telling me whether I'd won, the paper in the envelope told me whether my child would die. As a parent walks into these meetings, she knows the doctors are aware of what is written on that paper in the envelope. I always watched their actions and body language, wanting with all my might to both know and not know. I had never walked into a meeting with Dr. Weigel and heard good news, not once. However, I had to go. I had to watch the envelope open, and I had to hear what the paper said.

I tried to mentally prepare for any bad news. All three kids would be in the waiting room when we got the news because, coincidentally, we had tickets to the Twins game. It felt like foreshadowing. If it was bad news, I would just wait to hear what Plan E was, then work like hell to stay positive inside. Outside, I would be there for my three kids.

It was a good thing I prepared for bad news, because that was what we got. Scans showed a large tumor in Tucker's right lung, nearly a centimeter. Until this point, Tucker's biggest tumor had been ten millimeters, but now, in less than a month there was one nearly ten times that size. Tucker was not eligible for the immunotherapy trial that I hoped would be his cure.

The scans also showed that there was a lot of air in his left lung that needed to be fixed. He'd tried his hardest to recover, but now needed a procedure where he once again had to be put to sleep so doctors could work on his lung. They wanted to do it right then, but I asked if we could please go to the Twins game and do it tomorrow. This time I wasn't just advocating for Tucker; I needed to get the hell out of that hospital, as I was about to lose it from this devastating news. When the doctors saw that we were all dressed in Twins gear and Tucker began to cry about needing yet another procedure, they agreed that it would be better for him to have the fun night with his sisters and Mason at Target Field.

The procedure would require an overnight stay in the hospital. Normally just a one-night stay would not be too big of a deal, but this was the night before my wedding. Therefore, I would miss the groom's dinner. But Dr. Weigel said she would be able to get Tucker and me out of the hospital in time for my wedding Saturday afternoon. Then we should be able to relax on Sunday before heading back into the hospital for testing on Monday. The new chemo was planned to start on Tuesday. Friday morning, Tucker and I arrived to the hospital early, a first for us. He was put under at 7:50 a.m. for the fifteen-minute procedure where they inserted a chest tube into his left lung.

I wish Tucker could have napped all day, because when he woke up, he remembered the big family dinner we would be missing and started crying. This poor boy kept losing out on things, and now he felt bad that I was going to miss my own groom's dinner. I told him that we would have tons more family steak dinners. My heart broke as Tucker kept crying, "I'm trapped here!" Once again, the one baby bird stuck in the nest while all the other young birds flew to wherever they want to go.

Chapter Forty-Two

Saturday morning, Tucker and I left the hospital at 10:30, which allowed us to join in the wedding preparations. Tucker was happy because he hated missing the fun of A-Team events, and I was happy that I had time to get my hair and makeup done.

Kevin and I were ready and enjoyed our day. Tucker was the most handsome best man ever in his suit, tie, and top hat, while Kayci and Siera were beautiful junior bridesmaids in their fuchsia dresses. Dayra was my matron of honor. Tucker handed us our rings, and then Kevin and I were husband and wife. The emotional highlight was the mother-son dance that I enjoyed with Tucker. Despite not feeling well, Tucker found the strength to stand up from his wheelchair and sway with me. Then, he worked even harder and pivoted on his foot so we could turn and sway. I could see how hard he was working to make this dance wonderful for me. In the video of this moment, the guests' sobs were audible. Tucker and I had always had a special connection, but fighting this war against cancer together strengthened our bond to a level that was visible to everyone, especially during this amazing moment.

The whole day was full of love, family, and close friends. It was wonderful. Until it wasn't. Tucker was really hot and not feeling right, so after a few other songs we brought him inside the house to relax in the air conditioning. His little cousins came to be with him and keep him happy. Lisa told me to enjoy the reception and that she would take care of Tucker.

A couple hours later, she told me I had to call Tucker's doctor to report that his breathing was too rapid. Fifteen minutes later, I ditched my wedding dress for some leggings and a T-shirt, then loaded a sobbing Tucker into my car. I sat with him while Lisa drove us to the emergency room. Kevin stayed behind to entertain our guests. Tucker was bawling because he had to miss a party, just like the night before. It was surreal at this point that we couldn't even have one day of joy without something awful happening.

We were back at the hospital after only twelve hours of freedom. Tucker continued to be depressed as he lay on the hospital bed to get accessed while his sisters were having a fun sleepover at Grandma and Papa's. As for me, I stayed upbeat and told him he should be honored to be with the fanciest person in the whole emergency department. My hair was still in an updo with hot pink flowers in it, and my makeup held up pretty well in the heat. The doctors and nurses asked where we had been, then wished they hadn't when they learned I had just left my own wedding reception. It was fine, I told them, not wanting Tucker to feel any worse.

The X-ray showed that Tucker's lungs were fine; no problems from the procedure the day before. His fever was 100.9 and his white blood cell count was 13,000. That was outrageous—the normal range is between 5 and 11. That meant that the poor boy's body had been trying to beat an infection all day. Doctors confirmed that it had nothing to do with leaving early and agreed it had been the best thing for Tucker to spend the day with family at our wedding. They said it was just unlucky that he'd caught a "bug"—with so many things happening in his body, it just couldn't fight it. I was sad but grateful that Tucker had tolerated being so miserable so we could have our family wedding. Tucker hid his misery well, but thankfully Lisa knew what to monitor.

It took until 2:45 a.m. to get transferred to his room. Lisa insisted on staying, of course, but I told her to lie next to Tucker and nap with him while we waited to go up to Floor Five. Lisa helped us transfer Tucker into his bed, watched him fall asleep, and then went home. I took down my hair and put on some scrubs for pajamas. The nurse who gave them to me said, "Not the something blue you wanted, but here you go." I laughed. Definitely not the wedding reception and night I'd hoped for, but with cancer, nothing goes as hoped.

With antibiotics and lots of sleep, Tucker was feeling much better on Sunday. We relaxed all day, and evening brought lots of visitors. With so many people, it was like the wedding all over again. The nurses were now very used to this scene and knew exactly where to go to help us find extra chairs for all Tucker's guests. It was wonderful to be all together again and to hear Tucker laughing and playing. A mother can only take so many tears and sobs.

Chapter Forty-Three

The summer fun did not start as hoped. Tucker was very tired. Neither lung was strong or even fully healed yet from the surgeries, so he wasn't able to breathe well. Lisa was also extremely concerned that Tucker's weight had gone from sixty-three pounds down to fifty-two over the four weeks since the surgeries had started. Tucker wasn't eating and wasn't hungry. He was still taking a lot of oxycodone, which leads to constipation, so I started trying to get him to take medicine for that; however, those oral meds triggered his anxiety, which often caused him to throw up. Thus, even more weight loss. We were stuck in a mini perfect storm.

Tucker was able to make it to his playoff baseball game that week, despite needing to be on oxygen. This heroic teammate sat in his wheelchair with air tubes in his nose, feeling completely exhausted but still cheering on his buddies. It was heartbreaking and inspirational at the same time. That night I had promised Tucker would get his sleepover at Grandma and Papa's to make up for the one he'd missed after the wedding. Lisa was nervous about his condition, as was I, but we didn't want to take this away from him and his sisters. We agreed we would both stay awake and next to Tucker all night to monitor him. It was a scary and long night, but thankfully Tucker never passed a threshold of needing to go to the ER. Poor Lisa had to go to work while I took a nap when Papa and Grandma woke up to take care of my kids.

Lisa and I were making many calls and doing a lot of research to come up with a plan to treat Tucker's anxiety, keep oxygen on, get some food into him, and give him enough rest but also enough movement that his lungs could get exercise. We were in a black cloud of stress, worry, and hope while struggling to find a formula that would get Tucker's condition to improve.

Tucker was sick of lying down, so during the days he would sit up next to me and lay his head on my chest. Often, he would fall asleep on me, and I would softly rub his back and kiss his head. For as long as I live, I will never forget when he woke up from one of his naps and asked, "Mom, when was the last time I told you I love you?"

"What, honey?" I wasn't sure I'd heard him right.

"When was the last time I told you I love you, Mom?" Tucker repeated in a sweet, sleepy voice.

"Tucker, I know you love me."

"But when did I say it? I feel like it's been a long time since I told you I love you. I'm sorry if I haven't said it for a while," my amazing boy said to me.

"Honey, you tell me every day, and I know it even when you don't tell me."

"But I want to tell you. I'm sorry if I haven't told you today or yesterday. I love you, Mom."

"I love you more than you will ever know, my sweet, sweet boy. You are a perfect son, and you are my hero. Now just get some rest. Mama is right here holding you."

"I love you," he repeated, and then fell back asleep. I knew because, as my tears dripped onto his head, he didn't bother to wipe them off. I was blessed with an incredibly loving son.

Despite Tucker's condition, his doctors felt it was important to keep the chemo on schedule. So, on Monday the twentieth, I brought him to the Journey Clinic. That night I wrote this entry on CaringBridge:

It is 4:25 a.m., and I am going to sleep and will write more tomorrow. Tucker had T today as an outpatient. Then we ended up back here and getting accessed for the second time in ten hours. And admitted to the hospital three hours after that. I promised my mom I wouldn't swear in these entries. So, I need to wait until tomorrow to talk. I'm so mad at cancer right now I can't even deal.

I was just worn down from the frequency of bringing my son to the hospital, promising him a better day tomorrow, and that *never* happening. Since that playdate with Owen two weeks ago, Tucker had been accessed four times and had three trips to the emergency room. Our fun, hospital-free summer was anything but. At this point, Tucker was throwing up every eight hours, had no appetite, and couldn't get off the couch. He couldn't sleep well because the steroids he had to take spiked his anxiety. Tucker had to take ten doses a day of seven different kinds of oral medication. We were stuck in a cycle from hell.

I worked hard to take things one day at a time and focus on the little moments of joy and improvement, like Kayci sitting by her big brother, rubbing his head, and watching his TV show with him even though she didn't like it; he ate a piece of toast that Siera insisted on bringing to him. But deep down, I knew: for the first time, Tucker did not have quality of life.

One night as I was giving him a bath, being careful to avoid the new scars and saddened to see his ribs so prominent, I said, "I wish I could go through this for you."

He immediately responded, "I wish no one had to go through this." Tears fell as I sighed and nodded.

Chapter Fourty-Four

On Saturday morning, June 28, Kevin and I picked up the kids from Judd's house to bring them to Maetzold for Kayci and Siera's baseball games. I found out Tucker had a nosebleed and had vomited blood during the night. We brought him to the games hoping he would have fun, since he hadn't been outside all week. Once again, even my smallest wishes weren't coming true. During the ball games, Tucker's oxygen level declined and he had a light nosebleed. Then he got a headache, and I couldn't take any more. I wanted to scream, "*Why is this happening?*" right there in the middle of the ballpark. I left the games to bring Tucker to Kevin's air-conditioned house.

I called the on-call doctor and told him that if I saw one more symptom or deterioration, I would be bringing Tucker in, so he needed to let the emergency department know. I knew in my gut something was wrong, so I went into Lisa-mode and started making demands. Two minutes after I hung up, Tucker threw up blood and his nosebleed resumed. That was it—he was going in. I told Tucker, "I'm going to bring you to the hospital because they can fix you there. Mommy can't fix you here at home, and you deserve to feel better." For the first time, he didn't object, which catapulted my nervousness into pure fear.

I quickly cleaned up Tucker, simultaneously trying to slow down the nosebleed and figure out what to do with the girls. I had told them that I would be taking them to Target and spending lots of time with them all day. Cancer made me a liar, once again. When I told them I had to go to the hospital instead, they started crying, rightfully so. I decided that Kevin should follow through on my plans with the girls instead of coming with me and Tucker. I sent him off so Kayci and Siera wouldn't see the blood and get scared.

I quickly realized I'd made a mistake when I had to carry Tucker to the car. Kevin's house had a full flight of stairs with turns in it, and then more stairs down the porch. I picked Tucker up; he was so limp I thought he was asleep. I hardly made it all the way down the stairs. Only an adrenaline surge as I nearly collapsed enabled me to get him down the front porch and into my car. I nearly dropped him as I waited for that van door to slide open.

That drive to the hospital was the scariest twenty minutes of my life. Tucker was too tired to sit up, so he was lying across the seats with blood slowly trickling out of his nostril. I kept trying to talk to him, but he wouldn't answer. I thought my son was dying right in my back seat. My voice stayed calm even as tears streamed down my face; I kept asking, "Tucker, buddy, are you OK? Are you just tired?"

He didn't answer. I asked again, "Tucker, are you just tired and getting a little rest?" I kept watching in the rearview mirror while trying to maneuver through the tunnel and speed past the other cars. The calm barely stayed in my voice as I raised my volume: "TUCKER? BUDDY?"

Finally, I saw his head nodding. I asked again, "So you're just resting?" I have never been so happy to see a head move.

I was thrilled to finally see the colorful glass of the Masonic Hospital as I sped into the parking lot. I just grabbed Tucker out of the back seat and ran to the door, no time to waste on the wheelchair. I pushed through the doors, my son in my arms, blood trickling out of his nose and spots on his shirt. Holding back the urge to yell, "Save my son!" I used a firm and semi-loud voice to say, "This is Tucker Helstrom; his doctor called to tell you he was on his way. Where am I bringing him?" They said something about getting me a wheelchair for him and maybe something about an ID sticker when I firmly cut them off and said, "Open the doors and tell me what room I am bringing my son to."

The emergency department doors opened, and for the first time I was thankful to be there. As soon as I set Tucker on a bed, I held his hand and noticed my heart was racing and my arms were shaking. I worked to catch my breath as I silently told myself, *He is alive. Dana, he is alive. Just breathe.*

Lisa arrived very soon after us. I was so relieved she was there and could take over holding Tucker's hand and telling him he was going to be just fine. We switched roles, her taking that duty as I went out to talk to the doctors. I didn't want Tucker hearing all the horrible symptoms that had transpired over the last twelve hours. I demanded pain relief for his headache and fluids for all he'd lost throwing up, and I told them I was sure he would need a blood transfusion. My adrenaline had never surged more than it did at this time, but the doctors responded well to my tone and directions. They decided Tucker would get double doses of red blood cells and platelets, as both were nearly depleted.

Tucker slept the whole evening and night, except when he would wake up yelling that his head hurt. I would hold his head, trying to help him with the throbbing pain, but nothing helped.

I insisted that the doctors give him morphine along with his oxycodone because I had never seen him in this much pain from a headache. I hoped that as soon as he had enough fluids to rehydrate, the headache would subside.

As doses wore off, Tucker would yell in pain again. Luckily, a mother's touch and pressure could console him until it was time for the next dose of pain meds. It is amazing how much you learn about how your child's body works and how to help it. I was grateful to provide any help that made my son feel even a little bit better.

It took until 3:00 a.m., but finally all Tucker's vitals were vastly improved. However, he was still having headaches and his urine was still bright yellow, so I asked for more fluids, hoping that things would get better once he was rehydrated. It took until noon, but at last there were improvements in this area as well. Tucker slept for twenty-four hours, other than those bouts of pain and points where staff needed to wake him momentarily. He was still having headaches, but I thought they could be from not eating for the past thirty hours.

Tucker slept until 4:00 p.m. on Sunday and still hadn't eaten or drunk anything. The doctors suggested he stay, and I fully agreed. My family encouraged me to go to Kayci's baseball game; as scary as it was leaving Tucker, I knew it would be very helpful for Kayci and Siera to see me for a while. My brother-in-law, Cap, came to sit with Tucker.

Kayci loved having me there, and Siera sat in my lap the entire game. Of course, much of the A-Team was there to support Kayci and play with Siera. Kayci's team won, but I was too worried about Tucker to celebrate. While Kevin and the family took the girls out for ice cream, I sped back to the hospital, not even stopping by my house to pick up clothes. I knew my boy was missing me. It turned out that he had woken up before I had returned to the hospital and instantly started crying upon learning I wasn't there. Cap tried hard to distract him, but to no avail. I hated myself for leaving.

Finally, at midnight Tucker roused enough to ask if there were any waffles left. No, he was not hallucinating. At 2:00 p.m., he had said he was in the mood for waffles, but not from Perkins and definitely not from the hospital. He wanted Grandma's waffles. One text later, Grandma and Papa were hurrying around their kitchen packing up supplies, and within half an hour they were in Tucker's room. Tucker had fallen back asleep, but my mom had made a waffle right there in his room, hoping the smell would wake him up and he would finally eat. Grandma also brought a scrambled egg for him; unfortunately, I fed him that first. The bite of egg made him throw up. Papa and Grandma had left the waffle with Tucker, hoping he would try it eventually, but he never did and I'd had to throw it out.

But at midnight, that all changed. Forever the optimist, I'd had Grandma leave the waffle batter and iron with us. I jumped off the couch/bed, plugged in the waffle iron, and made a fresh, warm, delicious waffle. I turned on all the lights and let the waffle iron beep extra long to make sure Tucker stayed awake. I poured the syrup on and fed him. He ate a full half of a waffle! He didn't open his eyes, but when he was ready he'd open his mouth and I'd feed him another bite. It was wonderful.

After Tucker fell back asleep and I started cleaning up, my joy froze, just like when there is a bad internet connection. As I replayed the happy event of Tucker eating, it hit me: I was so excited over such a small, basic, everyday event. What was happening? My son was so sick that eating a half of a waffle was reason to celebrate. How depressing.

I could have stayed stuck there, but I didn't. I refreshed the connection and went back to enjoying the moment. Yes, this was unimportant in normal lives. But cancer wasn't normal, and for now, this was something to celebrate. My son was getting better, and someday we would remember that it all started from Grandma's waffle, made by his mom, while in the hospital at midnight.

As exciting as the waffle victory was, it unfortunately did not have the power to change the course for Tucker. He remained sleeping through midday on Monday, and still had no energy or desire to wake up or take meds. The doctors and I started talking about options for helping him more, since the blood transfusions, hydration, and rest weren't enough. I called Lisa so she could be part of the discussions too.

After a few conversations with different staff, I decided and Judd agreed to get a nasogastric tube placed. I would put all Tucker's medications, liquids, and nutrition into the tube so he would not have to take things orally. We thought it was the surest and fastest way for Tucker to gain weight, stay hydrated, and get all his meds. An added benefit was the reduction of his anxiety. I just hoped he wouldn't have further anxiety from his appearance and discomfort from the tube.

Tucker was very brave when the nurse placed the tube. We were lucky we could give him a triple dose of Ativan before the procedure. Tucker did well, but it did cause him to throw up. He would have to get used to the feeling of the tape and tube on his face. He slept most of the night Monday, but when he did wake up, he said he was not going to let anyone see him like this.

Other than that, Tucker was tolerating the tube well, and I was excited to be getting some Pediasure into him. I was only giving him an ounce every three hours, but at least it was something—until it wasn't. On his third dose, Tucker threw up, a lot. *Why? Why can't anything go smoothly? He just lost everything I "fed" him.* We'd been on schedule to get discharged the following day, but that now was in jeopardy. I just wanted my son to keep his nutrients and meds in so I could bring him home. How was that too much to ask for?

Chapter Forty-Five

Tuesday morning, Tucker was finally awake enough for our favorite, Erin the PT, to come have a session with him. Unfortunately, Lisa couldn't make it to this one, but there wouldn't be much movement; we were mostly working on him being awake and sitting up. Erin used all her motivational talk and positivity to convince Tucker he could get out of bed and over to the chair. It was a struggle; it caused me so much sadness to see how truly weak my son was.

Together we eventually got Tucker to the recliner, and Erin set out some dominoes for him. She wanted to do a little work with his fine motor skills. I was so excited to have Tucker sitting up and in the chair. He also talked more with Erin, and I was sure this meant he was rounding the corner and getting better. Maybe today would be discharge day, and together Tucker and I could go to Kayci's semifinal baseball game tonight.

I sat next to Tucker; Erin sat across from him and put the dominoes on the hospital tray-stand. She gave Tucker the direction to put the tile with the same number of dots next to the one she set out. He had four to choose from.

Tucker didn't respond. Erin repeated the directions, and of course I jumped in and said, "Just put the one with the five dots like this one, next to it." Another thirty seconds went by, and Tucker didn't make a move. He told me that I should just pick one. Erin and I stared at each other, utterly confused. Was he that tired?

I urged him to just move the domino next to the other one; I was so afraid he couldn't lift his arm. Finally, Tucker did lift his arm and went to reach for the tile, but he reached under the entire tray. Erin and I were completely baffled, and then I felt it slide into terror.

Erin was nervous too. She set out a different tile and said to just point at the domino that matched it. It took so long for Tucker to respond, and when he did, once again he pointed under the tray and not at any domino, let alone the correct one. We both managed a "Great job!" before I said I had to go to the bathroom.

I hurried out of the room and ran to the nurses' station. I told them I needed a doctor right now! My son couldn't see! I started crying and told them to please hurry and get me a doctor. I wanted to collapse right there. *Why can't my son see? Did he have a stroke? Does he have an aneurysm? What is happening to my child?*

But I couldn't collapse. In fact, I couldn't even cry. I knew Tucker was timing how long I was gone and was going to be studying my reaction to determine if he should be afraid or not. It was up to me to remain calm and positive. So I wiped my eyes and hurried back into his room. Erin was a rock, still chatting with him and telling him how proud she was of him for working so hard to get to the chair and get through all of these transfusions. It was working, Tucker seemed pretty calm and smiled as he received her praise.

Soon one of the doctors walked in; I greeted him and acted surprised. I wanted the doctor to see what was happening, so I told Tucker that this was the last round—he just had to point at one more domino. Erin set out a different tile and I said, "Just one more time—you're doing great, buddy! Point to the domino that matches this one."

Once again, Tucker's arm didn't get up to the table; he pointed at nothing, not even one of the choices. If I had any heart left, it disintegrated from heartache and fear. But not my voice. "Great job, buddy!" I sang out. "You did it!" Erin stayed and chatted with Tucker while I walked out to the hall with the doctor.

I refrained from yelling but was stern and panicked as I demanded, "What is happening to my son? Why can't he see or lift his arm?" Was this in connection with Tucker's terrible headaches? Did he have an aneurysm or brain bleed? I didn't even know the difference between those things, I just knew all of it was terrifying. I was not going to let this doctor go without answers. I told him I wanted Tucker to have a brain scan. My son couldn't see and possibly couldn't move his arm—this needed to be figured out.

The doctor tried to calm me down and told me that only 1 to 2 percent of the time does the brain ever get affected in osteosarcoma patients. He said they hadn't done any scans because it was much more likely that something else was wrong.

I didn't care about statistics at that point. My son was having everything go wrong, and it was time to check every possibility. The doctor read through Tucker's chart. He noticed the triple dose of Ativan that Tucker had the evening before for the NG tube, and told me that it was possible that the vision problems could be a side effect of all of the anti-anxiety meds in Tucker's system. His plan was to eliminate all anxiety meds today and come check Tucker in the evening when everything was out of his system. The doctor worked hard to reassure me that it was highly unlikely anything was wrong with Tucker's brain.

This answer sounded so good to hear that I accepted, but I told the doctor that I would be demanding action if any other issues arose. Also, if Tucker's sight and movements weren't completely better by this evening, I was not going to stop until I got him a brain scan. I took some deep breaths, reminded myself that this was highly unlikely, and went back into Tucker's room.

Erin gave me a huge hug before she left. She too knew something was wrong, seriously wrong. She told me she would call Lisa for me and tell her what had happened. That was wonderful, because I couldn't relive that without falling apart.

I wasn't surprised when Lisa was soon at our door, pleasant and positive as ever. She told Tucker how great he looked and how proud she was of him. He was still in the recliner, but Lisa suggested he would be more comfortable in bed. Tucker again responded to her praise with pride. She was his other rock, and he knew he could believe everything she told him. Lisa helped her nephew get back into bed and rubbed his head while he fell back asleep.

At that point, she turned to me and told me I'd done the right thing, and that she would help me get to the bottom of this. We couldn't say more—it was too scary and Tucker could be listening. Lisa gave me a hug and said she would see me later. Before she left, I went into the hall to call Judd and tell him what had happened. I told him he should get down here today and let him know what not to say or do.

Sitting alone in the room while Tucker slept, I replayed the last seventy-two hours in my mind. I realized that Tucker had said he was "too tired" to watch the Twins game with me Sunday evening. Maybe the truth was he couldn't see it? He had also been surprised when the scrambled egg was in his mouth. Had he not seen it on the plate or the fork before I fed it to him? *How long has this been happening? Why didn't my son tell me? Is he scared? He must be scared. Was he not telling me to protect me?* It was all so terrifying and painful.

Tucker napped most of the day. He woke up and talked to Judd a little bit, and was of course pleasant to the nurses when they stopped in to check his vitals. At 5:00 p.m., I made the incredibly difficult decision to go to Kayci's playoff game. Tucker was not in pain and seemed fine with Judd there. I could tell Kayci was getting more and more nervous the longer Tucker stayed in the hospital, and she must have figured something was wrong since I was not having her and Siera come visit very much. I decided it would be very reassuring to the girls if I left the hospital, and she would enjoy having me support her—and of course, Siera would love to sit in Mommy's lap for an hour. Before leaving, I made Judd promise that he would call me when the doctor came to recheck Tucker. I also made him promise to put the doctor on the phone with me.

I drove straight to Maetzold. Being there was harder than I'd anticipated because of all the wonderful families asking me about Tucker. "How is Tucker doing?" they would ask. In my mind, my answer was, *"I think something is wrong with his brain and he might be blind, or he might have had a stroke or maybe just too much Ativan? You know, just another day in the life of hell. How are you?"* I did not say that, of course, but could hardly keep back the tears. Thankfully, everyone picked up on my quietness and stopped asking.

I sat on the far end of the bleachers and buffered myself with Siera on my lap, a Diet Coke in my hand, and family all around me. Lisa had informed them of what happened that morning, so we were all pretty quiet, except when cheering for Kayci. We were loud and proud of my amazing daughter, who was suffering inside too.

During the last inning, I got a text from Judd that the doctors were in the room checking on Tucker. I jumped up and ran to the empty field so I could talk. Lisa followed me.

I asked Judd if they were doing the same activity with the dominoes so they could compare apples to apples. He said they weren't; they were just checking by asking questions. *Damnit! I knew I shouldn't have left this up to anyone else!* I had specifically left the dominoes there and wanted to see if the exact directions yielded a different result. Judd went on to say that the doctor felt there was some improvement from this morning, so he was going to hold off on ordering any scans. *WHAT? NO!* I demanded Judd put the doctor on the phone. Judd didn't want me yelling at the doctor, so he wouldn't.

At that point I did start yelling. "I WANT MY SON TO HAVE THE SCANS! I INSIST HE HAVE A BRAIN SCAN! YOU SAID YOU WOULD IF IT WASN'T FULLY BETTER, AND IT ISN'T! GET HIM THE SCAN!" Thankfully, Judd didn't hang up on me and the doctor was able to hear me. Judd told me to stop yelling—they were going to order the scan. "GOOD!" I yelled. "I will be right there!"

Lisa was on her phone about to call Judd and do the same thing I was doing, but stopped when she heard me yell. She told me she was getting her car and would drive us there. As she ran to her car, I went back to the field to say goodbye to the girls. Kayci was on deck. I didn't want to panic her or Siera, so I stood there and cheered. I don't know how I smiled and acted "normal," but I pulled it off.

Kayci hit the ball well, but it was caught. I gave Siera a hug goodbye, then stepped into the dugout to give Kayci a hug and ran to Lisa's car.

Chapter Forty-Six

At a couple points during the drive, I worried about the possibility that Lisa and I would be the next patients in the hospital. I was fine with it, though, because I had to be by Tucker's side during that scan. We made it there in one piece; I ran into the lobby and up to Floor Five only to find out that Tucker had already been picked up. Damnit! But the nurses knew I would want to be with him, and they had someone waiting to bring me down to the scan rooms on Floor Two. I started jogging and so did she, using her badge to open all the doors so I could get to my son. Tucker had never had a scan or any procedure without me holding his hand, and a brain scan sure as hell was not going to be the first.

I got in the room and instantly smiled and acted calm. "Hi, buddy! You are amazing! I am so glad we are going to get to figure out how to make you feel better with this scan. This won't take long, and then the doctors can give you the right medicine so you can come home! You got this, buddy! Remember, you are my hero and I love you so incredibly much!" The scan commenced.

It didn't take long; soon we were back up in Tucker's room, where Lisa and Judd were waiting. Tucker fell asleep, and the three of us waited in silence. When I'd asked the doctor that morning how long it would take to get results, I thought he'd said within an hour. I must have heard wrong, as it had been an hour and no one had even stopped into our room. I went and talked to the nurse. No information. Twenty minutes later, Lisa went and spoke to her again. No information. It felt like minutes were taking hours. Where was the doctor? Why wasn't anyone giving us the results? I felt bad that Judd was there alone, as Kris was with her family at her daughters' national dance competition out of state.

I sat in the bed next to Tucker, holding his hand and rubbing his head. It had now been two hours. It was 9:30 p.m. It is not possible to explain the thoughts that were racing through my mind.

Finally, the nurse told us that one of the fellows was on his way to come meet with us. What? Why a fellow? Why not whoever was working this shift? Lisa held my hand, and we waited some more. I had no previous experience with this, but I knew this was not good. Finally, at 9:50 the doctor arrived. We had to meet with him in a private consult room. I was right. It wasn't good.

I think he talked to us for five minutes. I honestly only heard one thing: "The cancer has spread to Tucker's brain."

Since I wasn't listening to what he was saying, I cut him off and asked, "So now what?" He explained to the three of us that there was a lot of pressure inside Tucker's brain—he needed to get to the PICU immediately to receive steroids all night, which would hopefully stop the swelling.

I did not ask what would happen if it didn't work, because I'd found a whole new level of resolve and determination. I don't know from where, and I don't know how. I cut off the conversation and started giving directions. "Let's get going. Judd, go back and start packing up the room without waking up Tucker.

Lisa, stay here while I call our siblings and parents. Dr. Sean, let the PICU know he is on his way. Lisa and I will be there in two minutes. Do *not* take Tucker down without me."

I made a group call to Mom, Dad, Kevin, Mark, Sara, and Ryan while Lisa held my hand. "Hi—it's not good news. Tucker continues to be one of a kind; the cancer spread to his brain." I was in complete robot mode at that point; no tears were falling, except from Lisa's eyes. I went on, "We need to get the pressure to stop, so he is on his way to the PICU to get steroids to reduce the swelling. I am sure that will work and Tucker will feel better. I will call you back when we get down there." I ended with, "I am fine." Hanging up, I hurried to be by Tucker's side and helped push his bed into the elevator, then watched them get him situated in the PICU. Judd was with me and Tucker while Lisa finished packing up our stuff.

When I was introduced to the charge nurse of the PICU, she explained that Tucker's situation was critical. I didn't have time for guessing or reading between the lines, so I bluntly asked her, "Are you saying my family should come see him right now?" I thought I was being a little extreme, as it was 10:30 p.m., but apparently I wasn't. She answered yes, they should come in—Tucker might not make it until the morning. The swelling had been caught before any rupture, but if the steroids didn't work to reduce it, it would kill him.

Instead of panicking, my first thought was that my tantrum on the empty field into Judd's phone had been the right thing to do. I had possibly saved my son's life. My second thought was to hurry and get on the phone. I made the same group call and gave more directions.

"Everyone needs to come here now. Sara and Ryan, I am

having Kevin bring Siera and Kayci in; your call on what to do with your children. Here is what we are telling the Littles. 'Tucker is mad at his mom for not letting you visit for two days, so he is refusing to go to sleep until she lets you come see him.' Mom, call Lisa's girls and Gregg and tell them to come to the hospital. Kevin and Dad, when you get here please go get all of our stuff out of our room on Floor Five and pack that into Dad's car since Kevin will have the girls to bring home. Kevin, please tell Dayra so she can come too." I ended with, "See everyone soon, and don't worry—I am fine and Tucker will be fine. I love you all." They all responded, "We love you too."

I hung up and went to tell Tucker the good news. "Hey, buddy, guess what. Sara, Ryan, and Kevin just called, and all the Little cousins are refusing to go to bed! They are mad that they haven't gotten to see you for a couple days and won't sleep until they get to. So they are coming in!"

For the first time in four days, Tucker smiled. A real, wonderful, and warm smile. Then he said, "I knew they were missing me."

"You're right. They miss you a ton. Everyone does, so they are all coming."

Tucker responded with one word: "Yay." I was thrilled that my son was feeling joy. I was also thrilled that I was numb and not feeling.

By 11:15 p.m., there was a party in the PICU. Tucker was in his bed, covered with a prayer shawl, surrounded by a ring of little cousins and a second ring of big cousins. The innocence and love of children is the most profound thing to witness. Kayci was beside him rubbing his head. His hair was starting to grow back a little, but it was still what Kayci always did whenever she was next to her best friend. Siera was sitting on his bed down by his foot and rubbing his leg. Tucker said, "I heard you missed me." And boy, did that trigger a lot of big responses, confirming how true that was. The big cousins continued the wonderful conversation while I asked my siblings to come to the doctors' meeting with me and Judd.

A neurosurgeon, an oncologist, and the PICU charge nurse were waiting in a small room; when they looked up and saw the eight of us, the nurse said, "I will find a bigger room." Yes, when one member of the A-Team is in need, a bigger room is necessary.

We all sat around a large table. I remember much of what was said here but will summarize, because really it all boiled down to two things. One: Tucker had started steroids; the team would take scans at 3:00 a.m., then again at 6:00 a.m. to see if they were working. If they didn't work, Tucker wouldn't make it through the night due to the pressure on his brain. If they did work, then the chief neurosurgeon would meet with us after the 6:00 a.m. scans to see if surgery was a possibility. Two: "This is a Do Not Resuscitate order. Dana and Judd, are you in agreement to sign it?"

I wasn't ready for that question. "*Do you want to let your son die?*"

Somehow, I was still very coherent at this point and asked about Tucker's lungs. Did they still have cancer in them? If so, how many tumors and how big? The oncologist said he didn't know because that hadn't been scanned. I told him that I wanted those scanned at 3:00 a.m. too. I did not want to put Tucker through risky brain surgery if his lungs were full of cancer that would kill him anyway.

They agreed to do the scan. Then I turned to Lisa. "Do I want to sign the DNR?" Judd agreed that he wanted to hear from Lisa.

Poor Lisa had the horrific task of explaining, yes—if Tucker did make it through the night but things got worse in his brain, he would still be not only blind, but even more miserable.

I didn't need to hear from anyone else. I looked at Judd and then asked for the papers. And signed them. This is what a mom does. Agree to have all the pain so her child can be free of it.

We walked back to Tucker's room in silence, and very much welcomed the chatter and laughter that were occurring there. However, it was now past midnight and time to get the children to bed. The parents arranged rides; Cap took the kids home so Sara and Ryan could stay at the hospital with me and Lisa. Mark took his kids Hailey and Henry home. Amy, Sophie, and Maggie helped Dayra and Kevin load up Kayci and Siera. I stayed with Tucker, right there in his bed with him. Judd tried to rest on the little sofa in the room between his check-ins with his son.

Tucker had to be given a cognitive test every hour. I hated having to wake him for their questions, but it was necessary to see if his brain was still working correctly. I did love one of the questions: "Who is with you?" the PICU nurse would ask. "Mommy," my boy would answer. My siblings sat in the waiting room together, coming in one at a time to check on me and Tucker, bringing me Diet Coke, and seeing if there was anything they could do. I held my boy all night and tried not to cry. I wanted to transmit only love and comfort. I think I kissed Tucker's cheek over a thousand times that night, each time hoping this one wouldn't be the last.

None of the kisses was the last one. Tucker responded well to the steroids and made it through the night. The 6:00 a.m. scans showed the pressure was relieved. I'd known deep down that he'd make it, but I was still glad everyone had come in to visit him. I have no doubt that helped him fight harder. I called my parents and Mark to let them know the good news. Ryan went home, knowing that I was in great hands with my sisters.

There was another meeting around 9:00 a.m. It took that long for the different doctors of the various departments to talk and arrive at their recommendations. Sara stayed with Tucker, always happily taking the jobs that let the "Batmans" do their work. Lisa, Judd, and I were waiting in another room for the physicians when in walked the chaplain to wait with us. I liked her very much, but I very much did not like that she was here now.

The oncologist, the nutritionist, and I don't remember who else came in to speak. I could guess the answer but asked anyway: "Why isn't the neurosurgeon here?" People were still settling into their chairs, but I didn't want to wait another second to know what the hell was going on with the cancer in my son's brain.

The oncologist explained that the bleeds in the brain were caused by lesions or tumors from Tucker's cancer, and that this was incredibly rare with osteosarcoma. There was that word again, "rare," like every phase of this war. They had only ever seen it spread to the brain a couple times before. I wanted to push with questions about why the surgeon was so sure he couldn't remove it, but stopped myself. Instead, I asked what the scans of the lungs showed. The oncologist just shook his head—probably the most powerful answer he could have given.

"So, it is back in his lungs again? Even more than the one tumor?" I questioned.

"It is all over his lungs," the doctor quietly answered.

God damnit, all this new chemo hell for nothing!

Back to the question I had asked so many times over the past eight months: "So now what?" Lisa held my hand, and I reached out to hold Judd's; I was hurting that he was all alone.

That was when Mary, the chaplain, started speaking. "It is time to put Tucker on hospice," she said, love and sadness in her voice.

I didn't like that answer one bit and didn't want to talk about it, so I moved on to the nutritionist. "Do we keep feeding him? Can he gain any weight and get healthier?"

"No, his body is shutting down and will not accept nutrition."

Still able to be pragmatic somehow, I asked, "Well if the feeding tube isn't helping, can we get rid of it?" Yes, we could.

Next question: "Can we keep him comfortable and pain free?" Mary and Lisa answered together: Yes, you can give him pain relief medications. To be honest, I don't remember how we did, and I never had to; Lisa and Sara took care of all of it.

With that done, I worked up the courage to ask: "How long do we have?" Luckily, I didn't have to be more specific.

One of the staff answered, "Days to weeks." I immediately thought I would contact his social worker to get something from Make-A-Wish done during that time—maybe a limo to a Twins game.

I only had one more question for the medical staff: "So when can I bring him home?" I don't know who answered, but they replied that I could bring him home tomorrow. "Why can't

I bring him home today? Tucker hates being in the hospital. You said we could keep him comfortable, so I want to get him out of here now." The staff looked at each other, discussed briefly, and then agreed that I could bring Tucker home today.

The medical staff left, but I asked Mary to stay. She sat next to me and held my hands. I looked her in the eye and very seriously asked, "Do you know if Tucker will be happy after he dies?"

Mary stared directly back at me and said, "Definitely. I know he will be happy. After death is a wonderful place, and everyone is happy there."

"Are you sure? I need to know my son will be happy."

This time, both Lisa and Mary chimed in, describing the beauty of the next phase of life.

"Do you know this for a fact, Mary?"

She remained patient and soft-spoken, but assured of her answers. "Yes, I have worked with people in hospice for over twenty years; I know this for a fact."

"OK, it's time to go bring my boy home to his sisters," I answered, and then hurried off to be by Tucker's side.

We went back to Floor Five to get the tube out and de-access. Upon leaving, I was swarmed with hugs and condolences from the entire staff. Everyone was in shock. No one had seen this before, and they couldn't believe what they had heard and read in Tucker's charts. It was good that I was so eager to get home, because I didn't have time to let myself consider that this would be the last time I would see these amazing, wonderful nurses and nurses' assistants. I hugged them on our way down the hall and off Floor Five forever.

On the way home, I texted Tucker's closest friends and told

them that he would be going to Kayci's game tonight. I hated that he wouldn't actually "watch" the game, but I knew my boy loved the sounds of a ballgame and friends. I was still determined to make him happy, not ready to give up on our motto. At Maetzold, Tucker was swarmed by people who loved him. He had to be reclining in his wheelchair with pillows tucked in to keep him comfortable, but he had his Hopkins little league hat and shirt on, along with his orange shorts. My boy found the strength to greet a few people and then hung out with Charlie and Greyson and all his friends from St. Michael.

I also sent a text to Carly, telling her things weren't good. Carly said she would pass this message on to Jason right away. He was in Las Vegas, where he grew up and his parents still live. I was sure that Carly would have Jason text or call Tucker, which I knew would make Tucker very happy. During Kayci's game, I got a text saying that Jason was getting on a flight soon so he could come visit Tucker tomorrow. *Wow, Jason Zucker is taking a red-eye flight to come see Tucker. I didn't even tell them he was on hospice.* I couldn't; my fingers physically could not type that word. I didn't know if they'd surmised it or what. Either way, it was quite exciting to tell Tucker that his friend Jason was going to stop by tomorrow just to say hi.

So far, I hadn't told anyone about hospice; not Tucker, not Kayci nor Siera. No one except the A-Team adults and Judd's family knew. This had been my first fear upon hearing the cancer diagnosis—well, my second. The first one was "What if he dies?"—after that was "What if I have to tell Tucker he is going to die?" As a school psychologist, I had told parents and kids bad news many, many times, but nothing this awful. I was going to need the next "days to weeks" to figure out how to do that.

Until then, I wanted to preserve any hours of joy for Tucker and all the kids that I could.

Worries about the message the kids would receive were what went through my mind when I typed this CaringBridge post Thursday morning, the day after we got home from Masonic:

Tucker did a great job in the ICU cooperating with the doctors and nurses, so they were able to find out what medicines would help him feel better. They found a steroid that would stop the swelling and gave him extra platelets to stop the bleeding! With all of that under control, I saw no reason why my boy shouldn't come home and join his family in watching Kayci's championship baseball game! So Tucker got to be down at his second favorite sports venue behind the Xcel, Maetzold ball fields! Kayci's team didn't win, but she won the contest of most fans with thirty-eight people there cheering her on! Thank you all for coming to support Kayci and visit with Tucker.

We will be keeping Tucker at home for now, while doctors consult. Judd and I and our families want to take this time to be together. Tucker is exhausted, but I am trying to make one plan a day for him so he can see people and they can see him. I know how very loved he is. I would like Tucker's friends to be able to see him, but he doesn't have enough energy to go anywhere. So tomorrow, Friday, July 1, I will bring Tucker outside to sit on the front porch from 3:00 p.m. to 4:00 p.m. if his friends want to come by and say hi.

Thank you for all the support. Team Tucker Go!

I wrote to convey to parents that it was serious, but to not scare any children. For once there wasn't denial, but I maintained my optimism due to my desire to protect everyone from the horrible reality that I had learned the day before.

Chapter Forty-Seven

With that denial and optimism, we went on to have a great day. I had changed Tucker into his Wild shirt to get ready for his special company. First, though, lots of cousins, aunts, and uncles came over, so it was a party, just like Tucker loved. The hardest part of the "party" was when Mason handed Tucker a picture he'd drawn and colored for him, like he had every single hospital visit.

Mason said, "I made my best picture yet for you!" Tucker reached out his hand; Mason didn't notice that he had to move the picture to get it to his cousin's hand. Sara and I froze. *Tucker can't see! How are we going to handle this?!* We should have known; we didn't have to. Tucker handled it perfectly, all on his own.

"Wow, that *is* your best one yet, Mason!" said my sweet, smart, and thoughtful boy, hiding his blindness from Mason and all the Littles who were gathered around.

Mason replied, "Well, I did have to take a break when I was making it."

"I would have needed two breaks," Tucker responded. "What's your favorite part?" Usually, Tucker pointed out his favorite parts of the picture, but he knew how to cover up his blindness.

"I like the tiger over here and the leopard over here," Mason proudly explained.

"I love those! You did a great job, Mason. Thank you for making it for me," gushed my dying, blind, nine-year-old boy. Sara and I had to leave the room, sobbing. Tears of pride and tears of pain, both for Tucker and for sweet little Mason, who was about to lose his best buddy.

The Littles ran off to play, and I came back to sit with Tucker on the couch. Soon we were greeting Jason and Carly. Tucker was propped up and rested enough to be able to talk. Jason sat right next to him, with Carly on his other side. Jason was amazing. He hadn't seen Tucker for a few weeks since they met for lunch the day Jason left for Vegas. Since then, Tucker had lost ten pounds and was very visibly sick. I later found out that they hadn't known Tucker was on hospice, so they were shocked to see him in this condition. That meant Jason flew here just to visit with Tucker and cheer him up since I said he wasn't doing well. He was even more wonderful than I already knew he was. So wonderful, in fact, that I have since told Jason that he is the man I hoped Tucker would have become.

Jason treated Tucker the same, talking about hockey and the Wild and even teasing him a little bit. Tucker of course teased him back, but not with his full force. He was on oxygen and exhausted, so his words were airy and brief. But he sure smiled. He knew Jason was next to him, at his house, and he loved him even more for it—as did we all. Tucker started falling asleep, so Jason and Carly made something up about how they had to get to a meeting.

Before they left, I went through Tucker's things and found his hockey picture from that season. A while back, Tucker had worked on writing his signature to be like Jason's, which is an artistic capital J and Z. Tucker practiced on regular paper; when he was ready, he used a sharpie, like Jason does, and signed the back of his hockey picture/card. "T. H. #16." It looked very much like Jason's autograph. I don't know how I remembered to look for this, but I'm so grateful I did.

As Jason was standing up to go, I hurried back into the room and said, "Wait, Tucker has something to give you!" Poor Tucker couldn't see what it was, so I explained, "Remember the hockey card you signed for Jason?"

I wasn't sure if he did, but Tucker answered, "Yes, make sure you give it to him." I did; Jason looked at it and got choked up. Then I told him to turn it over, and before I could even explain it, Jason recognized the similarity in the writing, and of course his number, #16.

I could see the tears coming to Jason's eyes, and so could Carly, prompting her to give Tucker a hug first so Jason could collect himself. Then he bent down, gave Tucker a hug, and said, "See you soon, buddy." All of us held in audible sobs, but tears rolled down every cheek in the room. Such a beautiful friendship that could have lasted a lifetime, cut short by damn cancer.

Jason and Carly left my house, but didn't make it far. I later learned that they sat in the car and cried. They knew they had just seen Tucker for the last time.

This hospice situation was getting more and more real, with the final goodbyes being made and Tucker sleeping nearly the whole time. Lisa learned all the necessary information from the hospice specialist on how to care for Tucker. I think there was a home hospice nurse assigned to us, but Lisa took care of all that so I could enjoy my last days with my firstborn child. Sara got some sleep the first night so she could stay the rest of the time and help Lisa with the around-the-clock care and monitoring.

I stayed on the couch, holding Tucker or sitting nearby while others sat by him.

Judd was with us and was happy to have his dad come down Wednesday and have Kris arrive Thursday evening. I was glad they were there for Judd. No parent should ever have to go through this, especially alone. Kevin opened his house to Judd so he could sleep there if he didn't want to go back to St. Michael. Judd's brother-in-law, Jeff, and the cousins, Anna and Maren, got home on Friday, then came straight to my house and spent the day around Tucker along with the rest of his loving family.

Chapter Forty-Eight

Friday, my house was the site of an all-day family gathering, just like it had been on Thursday. Aunts and uncles and the Big Five took turns watching over the Littles while they played in the sprinkler and whatever else they did. I sat with Tucker, and together we listened to the laughter and chatter that filled the air. Throughout the day, the kids would come over and talk to Tucker. Siera gave him a kiss on the head every time she walked by him; it had been their little game since Tucker lost his hair. Kayci would sit and rub his head, staying silent and forcing herself not to cry, but her eyes were full of love and sadness. It was time for me to tell the girls, but how?

Then I got a call from Dr. Weigel, so I went to my bedroom to talk. She had been out of town at a conference and didn't get to see us in person during our hospital crisis. She said wonderful things about Tucker and me and repeated how rare this was. You could hear the shock and the sadness in her voice. I can't imagine how hard it is to be a pediatric oncologist.

After hanging up with Dr. Weigel, I asked my mom to send in the girls. I shut the door and put them on the bed with me. "Girls, that was Tucker's doctor. She is very sad because she just told me that there are black Legos in Tucker's brain. No one knows why or how this happened; it wasn't supposed to. The black Legos in his brain aren't hurting him, but they are ruining his body." They asked what all this meant, so I had to say the words I hadn't said out loud yet to anyone. "It means that the black Legos are going to make Tucker die."

Even typing that word now is utterly difficult and extremely painful, but not as difficult as it was to say. And I am sure it was even more difficult for my eight- and six-year-old daughters to hear. They cried; I cried; then Lisa, Sara, and Grandma came in and cried with us. I don't know what my siblings said to their children; I was just sorry we all had to give this message and break the hearts of all of these young kids. Luckily, the commotion of a big family served as a distraction, which in tough times is wonderful. Mason and Olive wanted to show my girls something, so sooner rather than later they were back playing with their cousins.

We had people showing up to drop off food and sending lots of texts asking what they can do to help. There was so much love filling up the house; I knew Tucker could feel it, and it helped all of us be positive and strong. I was looking forward to welcoming Tucker's friends at three o'clock, like I'd mentioned in my post, but Lisa was very nervous. Friday morning, she had the unenviable task of telling me that Tucker might not make it that long.

What? What happened to "days to weeks"? This hadn't even been two days! I was angry and determined. I knew Tucker would want to "see" his friends one more time. I refused to take back my offer of having kids come see him. I kept the plan, counting on my son to hold on and be there for his friends. I was very worried about all these children who'd last seen him healthy. If they didn't see how sick he was, it would be harder for them to see that Tucker was miserable and weak. I wanted the kids to see for themselves that Tucker wouldn't want to be like this, to help them as they started their first battle with grief.

I did heed Lisa's warning insofar as making sure Tucker's closest friends came earlier than three o'clock. During the late morning hours, we had visits from Jayden and his family, Jack and his family, and Greyson, Charlie, Owen, Nolan, Weston, and their families. Everyone kneeled beside the couch as I sat beside Tucker and guided their conversations. All of the kids were wearing orange and Team Tucker wristbands. Then Señora Shrestha came over. I had always seen her love for Tucker, but it was truly palpable as she spoke to him. Her goodbye was as if she were saying goodbye to her own son. My heart broke for her as much as it did for the kids that were losing one of their closest friends.

Tucker was in a sea of orange love all day long. At three o'clock, the sea turned into an ocean. My parents went to the door and found a line not only to the sidewalk, but all the way down to the corner, children and parents wanting to come see their friend. Lisa was worried about how this would affect Tucker, so I promised her I would keep each visit short. Yes, this would be exhausting on Tucker's weak body, and he could no longer speak—his last full sentences had been to Mason and Jason the day before. But he could still smile softly, and that's what he did when he recognized every child's voice. Probably one hundred kids came through our house to say "hi" to Tucker. I hadn't told the parents that this would be goodbye; I didn't want the kids to be crying around Tucker. I wasn't sure if Tucker understood he was dying, but I was sure I didn't want him feeling like he made everyone sad.

By five o'clock, we had gotten everyone through. Tucker was

exhausted and sound asleep, but as I'd predicted, he'd fought to stay awake and hear each of his friends greet him. Now he could sleep, and I could feel good about giving my son the perfect send-off: family, Jason Zucker, baseball at Maetzold, and tons of friends. All while being held by his mom or dad, with lots of hugs from grandparents, aunts, and uncles, and snuggles from sisters and cousins. I was ready to let my son go be free from pain.

I told him that it was his turn to run and play baseball, and that is what I wanted for him. I will never know how I said those things and refrained from crying, but I am proud that I did.

That night Tucker wasn't ready to go yet, and I didn't mind one bit. I got into the corner of the couch Friday evening, with Tucker's head and chest in my lap. We were surrounded by family who were sharing memories and funny stories about our hero. Of course Tucker didn't want to leave yet; it was a party and he was the star. He loved making people happy and laugh, so I was sure he was loving the recap of just how many times he'd done that in only nine-and-a-half years.

That night, I took to doing what I do: worrying about everyone. I wanted to now post the reality of the situation on CaringBridge and help parents help their children through this. This is what I wrote:

Tucker Finally Wins

It was not the victory any of us wanted. But Tucker can finally win to get out of this pain. No more wheelchairs and missing legs. No more oxygen tanks and needles and shots. No more days and weeks lonely in a hospital. No more sitting on the bench when he should be the clean-up hitter or first-string defenseman. Tucker is about to win and get true happiness, which he hasn't had for over eight months.

Tucker's osteosarcoma spread to his brain. Something that specialists have rarely ever seen. It has been causing him pain over the past two to three weeks and shutting down his appetite. Apparently, this suffering wasn't a side effect from chemo. It was the damn cancer.

Sad for us, but beneficial to Tucker, is that there is no way to get it out of his brain. What's more, it also has continued to grow in his lungs. This demon tumor came straight at Tucker to defeat him. Little did it know, it had met its match and Tucker's spirit was stronger than the demon; Tucker's attitude was stronger than the demon; Tucker's personality and love for others beat the demon; Tucker's impact on others FAR outpowered the demon's impact. There is only one tiny way the demon was more powerful—and that was in Tucker's cells. That is the only place it won.

In every other way, Tucker beat this thing, and Tucker is triumphant in being the most amazing and heroic nine-year-old any of us will ever know.

I return to hold my son and have my family hold me as we say goodbye soon. But not forever, as he will be with me every day.

Love, Dana

Chapter Forty-Nine

I don't know where people slept that night, or even who slept in my house. I do know that I was on the couch with my arms wrapped around my son, and that Lisa and Sara were on the floor beside us taking turns checking on Tucker every thirty minutes. I was able to fall asleep holding my boy, a gift from my sisters, who did the worrying and monitoring for me.

I very vividly remember hearing Tucker's voice wake me up early Saturday morning. He hadn't spoken in thirty-six hours, but at 5:26 on Saturday morning, he said, "Mommy, lift me." I thought I was dreaming, but he said it one more time: "Mommy, lift me."

Tucker had never used that phrase before, so I quickly tried to figure out what he meant. I almost started to panic, thinking my son wanted something from me—what if I couldn't give it to him? But I took a breath and thought, *What would Tucker want right now? Oh!*

"Do you want me to lift you up so you can hug me?" My boy faintly nodded. He wanted to give his mommy a hug. I sat up, lifted him up, and placed my arms all the way around him. My sisters watched all this and took a picture of me, my boy, and our final hug. A priceless gift.

We were chest to chest, cheek to cheek, arms wrapped around each other. I hadn't realized how long it had been since we hugged. I hadn't realized how much better that was than just lying next to each other. But my son did. And he not only wanted it, he found the strength to ask for it. My son's dying wish was a hug from me. What an honor.

I held him for so long, telling him how much I loved him and how he was my hero. Eventually, I laid him back down, as he was already back asleep. Sara had woken up everyone in my house, and they all got to see this. I was not aware of any of that. At that moment, my entire world was Tucker and me—my firstborn, my only son, my hero, my heart.

Many of us thought that would be the end, but Tucker must have been so comfortable in his mama's arms that he stayed with us a little longer. We were all up and visiting in the morning, including Kayci and Siera, who came to sit with me and Judd on the couch. The Littles all stayed home with Katie and Cap that morning. My siblings, parents, and I knew it would not be helpful for them to see the final hours. I continued to tell Tucker how much fun he was going to have and that we were all proud of him. I told him I bet he would get to meet Jackie Robinson and play ball with him. I told him that I would always love him and be with him, but I don't think he ever doubted that. I also said I would be OK; I doubted that tremendously, but I didn't want Tucker to know that. Most importantly, I told him I would always take care of his sisters for him and make sure they were happy.

A little before 10:00 a.m., Lisa called my name and then pointed to Tucker. His chest wasn't moving, so I leaned down to listen; no air was coming out of his mouth. Tucker left this earth so peacefully, in a room full of love and in his mother's arms. A mother couldn't ask for a better send-off.

I continued to hold him as we all shared yet more stories

about our amazing Tucker. When I was ready, Lisa made phone calls and completed paperwork. We recorded the time of death as 9:51 a.m., July 2, 2016. I sat there holding my boy, trying to memorize the feel of his skin, knowing that I would never get to touch him or kiss him again. As I handed Tucker off to Judd, who brought him out to the vehicle that was waiting for him, I focused on Tucker's last request: "Lift me, Mommy."

I will, my sweet boy. I will lift you to be the orange sunset in the sky. I will lift you to be an inspiration for others. I will lift you to watch over me and your sisters. I will always and forever lift you and carry you in my heart.

Epilogue

On Thursday, July 7, we held Tucker's Celebration of Life in the Hopkins Pavilion, which had served as Tucker's hockey rink when it held ice during the winter months. It was the perfect venue to celebrate my son, and luckily big enough—we were honored to have over one thousand people attend. The following day, we held Tucker's funeral at St. Andrew's Lutheran Church, where over eight hundred people came to celebrate my wonderful son.

Six months after Tucker died, I started my nonprofit organization, Team Tucker: Play Laugh Love. I was determined to extend the legacy Tucker started and let my son's name, memory, and goodness live on. For four years I spoke of his heroic goodness and strength and pushed aside any compliments directed toward me. I believed Tucker was the example the world needed, and thus created Tucker's Sandlot and Tucker's VIP programs to help kids, like Tucker always did.

After Tucker's death, I was professionally stuck. I left my position at ISLA and was able to take a year off thanks to Kevin. I knew I didn't want to go back to teaching, but couldn't figure out what I should do professionally that also accommodated my need to be constantly present in Kayci's and Siera's lives. They needed me more than ever, and I needed them. Eventually I was working three part-time jobs during the times when the girls were in school or at their dad's, all while running and growing

Team Tucker and helping hundreds of kids. I knew I wanted to help others, but didn't know how to earn money doing that.

Then I was suddenly single again, as Kevin decided our marriage wasn't making him happy. My top priority being my two living children and the legacy of my dead child left too little for him. Every marriage is hard, but when a child dies twenty-one days into a new marriage with a blended family, it is extremely challenging. Then the COVID-19 pandemic hit. Now I was single, had lost two of my three jobs, and was physically cut off from my A-Team family, alone to financially and physically take care of my house as well as the educational and emotional needs of my daughters, who had just lost another family member.

That is when I turned to Tucker, who is like a guide for me now. I heard my son's voice telling me to "focus on you." I was scared by that message, because my passion was running Team Tucker: Play Laugh Love—he was the inspiration for that, not me. I was also confused because I didn't see what I added to this world other than sharing Tucker's story.

Tucker's voice told me to "write a book." Because I had a quiet home on the weekends while the girls stayed at their dad's, and because I needed to create a source of income, I went into Tucker's bedroom and started writing this book. I started with the intention of having one more way of sharing the story about my heroic son. However, by the end of the extremely painful process of reliving the most horrific days of my life, Tucker's first message now made sense to me.

Since November 4, 2015, I'd only seen Tucker as the focus of our journey, with Kayci and Siera being the two other main characters. As I retold the story, a different protagonist emerged:

me. The mom. The sun giving the strength and energy to the three planets revolving around me and the numerous satellites surrounding them. The marionette master pulling the strings of the doctors, still recognizing she knew her child's needs better than anyone else. The determined optimist who refused to let herself or her son be victims and instead convinced him there was nothing they couldn't do. Then it dawned on me: Tucker was the inspiration to help children, but perhaps I could inspire and help parents.

Already I have had the opportunity to help another mother as she signed the DNR for her three-year-old son. To help a father get a rental car so he could bring his son's casket back home several states away from where he died at a Twin Cities hospital. To counsel parents upon learning of their children's cancer diagnoses. I was able to help these parents in their worst times because I had been through a similar war.

The hardest thing I've had to do in my lifetime was this journey with my three children through Tucker's war with osteosarcoma. Now, I am realizing that every time I can help another parent in their war, it makes mine a little more palatable. It gives some justification for why I had to go through it. And it takes away an ounce of the massive pain I suffered and still carry. I hope this book reaches parents everywhere, and that when parents are suffering, they can reach out to me or my story for support.

I still deem being a mother the best thing that ever happened to me and the favorite part of my life. Tucker's death hasn't changed that. Actually, it strengthened my appreciation of getting to be a mom. Often I see things that make me realize I am more grateful to have two of my kids still alive than some parents who have all of their children. People forget that healthy children are a gift, not a given.

I am also grateful that I feel Tucker's love every single day and truly know he is around me, Kayci, Siera, the A-Team, and his friends, watching over us and helping us have strength to feel joy. I believe I was Tucker's source of strength while he was living, and I know he is my source of strength now. I feared death my whole life. I feared childhood cancer since the day I became a mom. It turned out that both happened to my first-born child. Both of my biggest fears came true. I am proud of myself for surviving all this and want to use my pain to help others survive too.

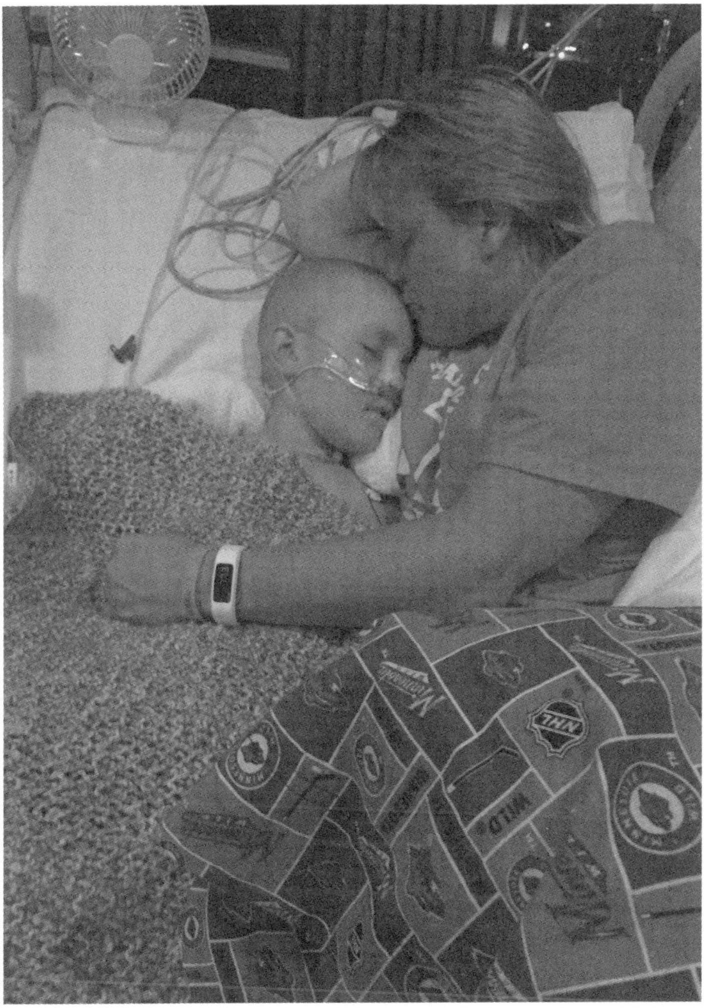

ABOUT THE AUTHOR

Dana Anderson-Helstrom is the executive director of Team Tucker: Play Laugh Love, a nonprofit organization that helps children battling life-threatening illnesses by getting their loved ones by their side. As a school psychologist, special education teacher, and soccer coach, she honed her gift of working with kids and families facing challenges. With a combination of empathy and problem solving, Dana helped numerous students achieve success and happiness. In 2015, Dana faced her own horrific challenge: her son's cancer diagnosis.

Since then, Dana has altered her career path to helping kids through Team Tucker and helping parents through Dana Cares, LLC. She is a speaker and author who inspires, counsels, and listens to parents confronting challenges.

Together with her daughters, Kayci and Siera, Dana lives in Hopkins, MN. They continue to be surrounded with support from their community and family and are watched over by Tucker, who is forever present.

www.PlayLaughLove.org

www.DanaCares.org